Bringing Policies to Life: The vital role of front line managers in people management

Sue Hutchinson

John Purcell

Acknowledgements

Once again we are deeply indebted to the senior HR managers and executives in the 12 organisations involved in this study (listed at Appendix 1), to the front line managers we interviewed and to the many employees who took part by answering our questions not just once but twice.

Our thanks also go to Konstantinos Georgiadis, a doctoral student at Bath University, who showed great patience and perseverance in helping us with some of the more complicated statistical analysis.

Bringing Policies to Life: The vital role of front line managers in people management

Sue Hutchinson

John Purcell

Work and Employment Research Centre,

School of Management, University of Bath

© Chartered Institute of Personnel and Development 2003

First published 2003
Reprinted 2004

Cover design by Curve
Designed and typeset by Beacon GDT
Printed in Great Britain by Short Run Press

British Library Cataloguing in Publication Data
A catalogue record for this book is available from the British Library

ISBN 1 84398 053 3

Chartered Institute of Personnel and Development,
CIPD House, Camp Road, London SW19 4UX

Tel: 020 8971 9000
Fax: 020 8263 3333
Website: www.cipd.co.uk

Incorporated by Royal Charter. Registered charity no. 1079797.

Contents

List of tables and figures   vi

Foreword   vii

Executive summary   ix

Chapter 1   Introduction – Understanding the role of front line managers   1

Chapter 2   The importance of front line managers in people management   11

Chapter 3   Where do front line managers make a difference?   25

Chapter 4   Managing the managers   45

Chapter 5   Practical implications   57

Appendix 1 Case study organisations – brief profiles   61

Appendix 2 Variables used in statistical analysis   69

References   73

List of tables and figures

Chapter 1

| Figure 1 | The People and Performance model | 2 |

Chapter 2

Figure 2	What employees think of front line managers' leadership activities by company	12
Table 1	Correlations between 'Relationship with FLM' and employee outcomes Leadership activities by company	14
Table 2	The association between 'Relationship with FLM' and employee attitudinal outcomes	15
Table 3	Correlations between teamworking, job discretion and 'Relationship with FLM'	18
Table 4	Tesco: Four stores compared in terms of leadership, job influence and commitment	19

Chapter 3

Table 5	Correlations between 'relationship with FLM' and HR activities	26
Table 6	The frequency of formal performance appraisals, as reported by employees by company	27
Table 7	The purpose of the performance appraisal scheme, as reported by employees by company	28
Figure 3	The provision of coaching and/or guidance by front line managers	32
Figure 4	Differences between occupational groups in the provision of coaching and guidance	32
Table 8	Correlations with the provision of coaching and guidance by the line manager	33
Table 9	Policy and practice of employee involvement schemes (other than teamworking) in selected organisations	36
Figure 5	Consultation by front line managers	37
Figure 6	How good are managers at involvement and participation?	38

Chapter 4

Table 10	The relationship between HR policy and practice, satisfaction and attitudinal outcomes for front line managers	47
Figure 7	The critical determinants of organisational commitment for front line managers	48
Figure 8	The critical determinants of job satisfaction for front line managers	48

Foreword

This Executive Brief draws on the data generated and reported in the CIPD research report *Understanding the People and Performance Link – Unlocking the Black Box* to further discuss the issue of front line leadership. The people and performance research, carried out for the CIPD by Professor John Purcell and his team at Bath University, identified a number of issues as being of particular importance to the relationship between people management and business performance.

They discovered that front line leaders are often crucial in making the difference between low-performing and high-performing firms. Occupying a key position in the organisation they are the deliverers of success by implementing strategies which focus the efforts of individuals on business goals and translating them into positive outcomes.

More and more front line leaders are active at the delivery end of people management. As a result the way in which they interpret and use the policies and practices designed by HR professionals has become an important determinant of the success or failure of those practices. The People and Performance model developed by the Bath team clearly places front line management as central to delivering business performance.

Drawing on the extraordinarily rich data generated during the three years of this study, the team has been able to develop a number of further insights into the nature of the front line leadership role which are reported here.

This is the first in a series of Executive Briefs which the CIPD plans to publish exploring in greater depth some of the issues raised by the People and Performance work. We hope these will offer insights for practitioners and enable them to more successfully implement the results of this research programme.

Angela Baron

Adviser, Organisation and Resourcing
Chartered Institute of Personnel and Development

Executive Summary

In May 2003 the major study undertaken by the University of Bath on behalf of the CIPD – *Understanding the People and Performance Link – Unlocking the Black Box* – highlighted the role of front line managers (FLMs) as crucial to the relationship between people and business performance. Front line managers are defined as managers who have first line responsibility for a work group of approximately 10 to 25 people. They are accountable to a higher level of management and are placed in the lower layers of the management hierarchy, normally at the first level. For example, in the Nationwide Building Society the relevant group studied comprised senior financial consultants responsible for sales teams, and in the Royal United Hospital (RUH) it was ward sisters.

This Executive Brief looks in greater depth at this issue and offers insights into the design and development of the front line manager role. In particular it analyses the impact of front line leadership on the components of organisational success.

Team leadership is an important aspect of motivating and managing people in all the organisations studied, and the leadership skills required the use of what are sometimes called

'soft' skills such as communication, involving, listening, asking and problem-solving. FLMs are often required to implement policies such as appraisal or team briefing and therefore had a significant role in 'bringing them to life'.

Leadership plays a significant role in influencing employees' attitudes towards the organisation and their job, and FLM behaviour is the most important factor in explaining the variation in both job satisfaction and job discretion or the choice people have over how they do their jobs. It is also one of the most important factors in developing organisational commitment.

There is a strong relationship between employee perceptions of front line management behaviour and the practices FLMs are required to implement, such as coaching and guidance, involvement and communication. Any improvement in FLM behaviour when implementing such policies may be associated by employees with an improvement in overall conditions and hence satisfaction with them.

However, there is also a clear gap between formal policy statements and practice – the rhetoric–reality gap. This demonstrates the impact FLMs can have on the outcome of policies. The way in which they are managed and developed is therefore crucial in influencing their discretionary behaviour, or the extent to which they are prepared to invest effort in their role, positively or negatively. The policies that are most supportive of line managers are:

◘ ensuring good working relationships with their managers

◘ providing career opportunities

◘ working to support their work–life balance

◘ allowing them to participate and feel involved in decisions

◘ having an open organisational culture which allows them to raise a grievance or discuss matters of personal concern

◘ giving a sense of job security.

The effort invested in managing front line leaders is vital because it is these individuals who make the difference to the way in which individual employees do their jobs, and hence to overall organisation performance.

Chapter 1

◘ **Defines the role of front line managers**

◘ **Describes their responsibilities and how they relate to the people and performance model**

1 | Introduction – Understanding the role of front line managers

In May 2003 the report of a major study undertaken by the Work and Employment Research Centre at the University of Bath, *Understanding the People and Performance Link – Unlocking the Black Box*, was published by the CIPD, which had funded the research over a three-year period. The report looked in detail at the way 12 organisations sought to manage their employees so as to have a positive impact on organisational performance.

Three main conclusions – from a complex and rich research project with many implications – were reached.

◘ First, organisations with strong values which were clear, widely understood and linked to appropriate metrics were more successful in getting commitment from employees.

◘ Second, it was the way that policies were implemented and enacted that was vital, and it was worse to have an ineffective policy than no policy at all.

◘ Third, the role of front line managers (FLMs) in bringing policies to life and in leading was among the most important of all factors in explaining the difference between success and mediocrity in people management.

This report looks in more detail at the front line manager role and the way FLMs have such an influence on employees and the way they, in turn, work productively and flexibly.

It is essential to understand why people management impacts on performance because without such an understanding it is impossible to appreciate the impact of FLMs. The full report of the project (Purcell *et al*, 2003) provided the theory and rationale for discerning the link between people and performance. In diagrammatic form this is the People and Performance model reproduced overleaf (Figure 1).

At the heart of the model is the focus on Ability, Motivation and Opportunity, known as AMO. In brief, all organisations – but especially those that aspire to excellence – have to be able to recruit and develop people with requisite ability, and to keep them long enough to reap effective work. But people with these abilities need some form of motivation to persuade or induce them to work effectively and appropriately. To do this they also need opportunities – opportunities to use their skills and competence in well-designed jobs, and opportunities to play a wider part in ensuring team and wider group success by being involved.

Figure 1   The People and Performance model

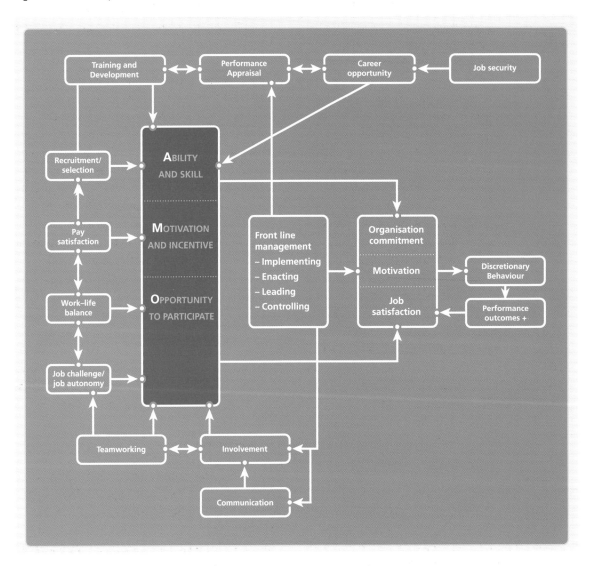

As we show in the report, achieving a right mix of AMO policies is as important for FLMs as it is for employees. Indeed, it is probably more important, given that these managers play such an important role in getting their team members to perform.

AMO is important because of its links to appropriate behaviour in the workplace in the way people do their jobs. Nearly all jobs have some element requiring the job-holder to choose how well, and how, the job is to be performed – for example, in dealing with customers. We call this 'discretionary behaviour'. Organisations that can trigger valued discretionary behaviour from their employees do better than others, and FLMs play a major part in this, as we show in the report.

Why and when do employees give discretionary behaviour? Many years of research, referred to in the main report, show that the prime link is with people's view of their employer. If they like working there, are proud to tell people where they work, and share the values of the employer – that is, they have organisational commitment – they are more likely to engage in making their job bigger by taking on more responsibilities and doing extra things.

The same is true of people who get high levels of satisfaction from doing their job – who are motivated. HR policies of the sort shown around the outside of the model are designed to maximise the whole and the parts of AMO, and this feeds directly into commitment, motivation and job satisfaction. So, as we showed in the main report,

these 11 policy areas are important. But because every organisation can have these policies there is no particular advantage to be gained – except that not having them is likely to lower performance.

What makes a difference – what we call 'organisation process advantage' – is the way these policies are implemented. This is where FLMs, and line management more generally, are of such importance. In the model we show this as Front Line Management; Implementing, Enacting, Leading and Controlling. The way FLMs carry out these activities is directly related to the levels of commitment, motivation and satisfaction that employees report, and this, in turn, is linked to the vital area of discretionary behaviour.

> *'Organisations that can trigger valued discretionary behaviour from their employees do better than others ...'*

We look below in more detail on how this is done, some of the difficulties in doing so, and how these managers themselves can best be managed.

Research methodology

Our study focused on 12 organisations from a wide range of sectors including manufacturing, retail, finance, professional services, IT and the NHS (see Appendix 1 for further details). In each case we selected a unit of analysis. In Nationwide, for example, this was a regional sales force; in the RUH it was a clinical department; and in Selfridges it was the Trafford Centre store in Manchester.

In each unit of analysis we conducted detailed face-to-face interviews with front line employees using a structured questionnaire which helped us explore how people management practices impact on employee attitudes and behaviour. These interviews were repeated 12 months later so we were able to track any changes in attitudes and behaviours.

This interview data was examined alongside data from interviews with senior decision-makers and front line managers, performance data and information on company HR policies.

A sister project investigating similar issues was conducted alongside this one, researching small knowledge-intensive firms over one year (Swart *et al*, 2002). Data from this study has been used in our analysis in Chapter 4.

Who are the front line managers?

We define FLMs as managers who are responsible for a work group(s) to a higher level of management, and who are placed in the lower layers of the management hierarchy, normally at the first level. They tended to have employees reporting to them who themselves did not have any management or supervisory responsibility and were responsible for the day-to-day running of their work area rather than strategic matters.

In our organisations spans of control would normally be between five and 20, although at the RUH and Selfridges it could be as large as 30

staff (including part-timers). At Selfridges, Clerical Medical, Contact 24, and the Royal Mint these people were referred to as 'team leaders', and at Jaguar 'group leaders' (one level below the supervisor). In Nationwide the individuals in our unit of analysis were 'senior financial consultants' (SFCs) responsible for sales teams, and at the RUH it was the ward sisters. At Tesco it was the section manager, a first line manager position.

In two organisations, however, where front line staff were members of multiple teams, there was no traditional FLM role and it was harder to identify a FLM position although day-to-day contact was with project managers. In PWC (see below) this problem was heightened by the fact that employees 'senior associates' could have up to six different project managers in any one year.

These individuals potentially occupied a difficult position. On the one hand, they were expected to be the voice of management and yet on the other the champion of the team's interests (Boxall and Purcell, 2003; p.110). As one group leader remarked:

You are the piggy in the middle.

In some organisations these FLMs had deputies, but this was normally a temporary position occupied by a potential team leader.

It was evident that in many firms the FLM's had been promoted from the ranks and most were unlikely to be able to progress much further in the organisation, as discussed in Chapter 4. Because of this they often fall outside management development schemes.

Our research shows how important these FLMs are in delivering effective people management. We explore this in this report by firstly looking at their role and importance. In Chapter 3 we look in detail at their HR activities, and in Chapter 4 on how they themselves are managed and motivated. Chapter 5 considers the practical implications.

Roles and responsibilities of FLMs

The responsibilities of FLMs covered a wide range of duties, ranging from traditional supervisory duties – such as work allocation and monitoring quality – to newer management activities, such as people management. In some cases it included cost control/budgeting.

The role typically included a combination of the following activities:

◘ people management

◘ managing operational costs

◘ providing technical expertise

◘ organising, such as planning work allocation and rotas

◘ monitoring work processes

◘ checking quality

◘ dealing with customers/clients

◘ measuring operational performance.

> *'Our research shows how important ... FLMs are in delivering effective people management.'*

Our concern in this report is with the people management role, and in all our organisations the most common activity handled by FLMs in this respect was absence management. This could include not just monitoring absence and lateness but also phoning (and even visiting) absent staff at home, conducting back-to-work interviews, counselling staff and conducting disciplinary hearings.

In other words, in some organisations FLMs were taking on much more of a welfare role – something done earlier by the personnel department.

Other people management activities frequently dealt with by the FLM included coaching and development, performance appraisal, involvement and communication (thus providing a vital link between team members and more senior managers), and discipline and grievances – all of which are discussed in more detail in Chapter 3.

In many organisations recruitment and selection was also carried out by the FLM, often in conjunction with the HR or administrative department (see the Selfridges case study). At Nationwide a pool of FLMs (senior financial consultants) were involved in interviewing prospective financial consultants, together with someone from personnel – a process that took place two or three times a year.

In the two organisations with multiple teams – PWC and ait – many of the people management activities were shared between different managers. At PWC, for example, project managers (and an individual could report to up to six different project managers over a year) were responsible for day-to-day supervision of a project and appraising the performance of team members, but overall responsibility for the annual performance reviews (which was linked to pay and development) and mentoring was that of 'counselling managers' (senior managers). Communication and involvement however (other than on day-to-day project matters) was handled by group leaders (again senior managers) and peer-group leaders.

Thus, in all our organisations FLMs were carrying out activities which traditionally had been the bread and butter of the personnel or HR department.

> **'Team leadership is an important aspect in ... motivating and managing people, ... a key aspect of the FLMs' duties.'**

Team leadership is an important aspect in terms of motivating and managing people, and in all our organisations this was a key aspect of the

FLMs' duties. (None of the teams we studied was 'self-managed', and few could be described as semi-autonomous.) As we suggest later in Chapter 2, how FLMs exercise their leadership skills in terms of managing the team could have a significant impact on the strength of teamworking and employee attitudes. These leadership roles required the use of what are sometimes called soft skills and are very much part of the 'doing' of management such as communication, involving, listening, asking and problem-solving.

In terms of people management the FLMs were often required to implement formal policies like appraisal or team briefing. But the main part of their role, and their major influence, was carrying out or 'enacting' the policies – 'bringing them to life' – particularly through their general leadership behaviour. In addition they had control of issues like quality and over some aspects of team performance, planning, work allocation and other activities outlined earlier.

The duties of FLMs are therefore larger and encompass far more responsibilities than the traditional supervisory role. The reasons for this expansion of the role have been much written about – organisational restructuring and the consequent decline of the middle manager, the growth in teamworking, increasing recognition that responsibility for managing people rests with the line rather than with a specialist, and the move to leaner methods of working. These changes undoubtedly place an increasing workload on the FLM, particularly when the 'newer' roles may have been taken on without relinquishing the old roles.

A distinguishing characteristic of FLM's in most of our organisations was that as members of the team they were also team workers, doing the same work in addition to their 'management' duties. Even if this was not part of their job, when staff were absent they often had to work on the shop floor, filling the vacancy on a temporary basis.

The pressures were often commented on by FLMs:

You never get anything completed. There's so much to do, covering areas … doing the work of my team.

It feels like a treadmill at times. I have a lot of staffing issues, trainees and absentees … It's about keeping your head above water.

And as one employee said of team leaders:

They spend less time on the shop floor and more time doing paperwork and 'the boards'. It takes over – no one seems to see them any more. I know it's not their fault. They are told to do it by their bosses.

Selfridges team leader role

The retail operations team leader (TL) position was re-defined in 2002 to give greater clarity to the role and more responsibility for people management activities. The main purpose of the role is to 'motivate, develop and lead the team to deliver excellent customer service and standards'. Key accountabilities cover four main areas:

- ◘ ensuring excellent customer service – including dealing with customer complaints, ensuring that sales associates (ie team members) understand the services offered, including the Selfridges account card

- ◘ the management of sales associates – for example, performance management (including absence management), liaising with team trainers, recruitment and selection, conducting disciplinary meetings

- ◘ ensuring effective communication and team working – including communicating on a daily basis with team members, attending weekly management meetings, planning weekly rotas

- ◘ ensuring excellent standards on the shop floor – for example, ensuring that all staff wear badges and adhere to the dress code, conducting refunds and exchanges, ensuring that the shop is tidy and clean.

Team leaders are also responsible for key performance indicators (KPIs) which are incorporated into their performance reviews and include such measures as stock control, mystery shopper results, rating the department on tidiness and cleanliness and, until recently, labour turnover. The key skills demanded of TLs include communication, being a team player, resilience, coaching and ability to motivate others.

One recent change has been the involvement of team leaders in the recruitment and selection process, formally a task undertaken by the HR department. Vacancies are notified by TLs to a central team located in Leicester who carry out an initial tele-screen interview based around values and behaviours. Successful applicants are then interviewed by team leaders who conduct an interview and advise on the job evaluation. The decision to select rests with the TL.

The whole process has been a success, improving the quality of recruits and, as one senior manager explained,

forcing the team leaders to be more disciplined, more planned, and forcing them to be less reactive … partly because the HR team are no longer available on site to wipe their backsides.

Chapter 2

◆ **Defines 'discretionary behaviour'**

◆ **Examines the relationship between front line managers and performance**

◆ **Explains the role of front line managers in managing teams**

2 | The importance of front line managers in people management

In our first report we maintained that one of the keys to managing performance through people is triggering discretionary behaviour in employees so that employees go 'beyond contract' or that extra mile for the organisation.

What we mean when we talk about discretionary behaviour is the choices people make about their work, such as in the range of tasks to be done, the pace at which to work, and how the work is to be done, covering such aspects as speed, care, attention to quality, innovation and style of job delivery. So, for example, triggering discretionary behaviour in a positive way could mean helping new starters learn shortcuts in their jobs, or sharing new ideas on work processes with team colleagues, or suggesting improvements at the workplace.

People are more likely to engage in discretionary behaviour when they feel motivated, are satisfied with their jobs and are committed to their employer – and here people management or HR policies and practices play a key role in terms of making the work and the working environment satisfying and motivating.

We also argued that front line management or leadership played a pivotal role in terms of

implementing and enacting HR policies and practices since it is the front line managers that 'bring policies to life'. Employee discretion is therefore affected by the way in which FLMs exercise their own discretion in terms of how they manage people. Employees are more likely to go beyond contract if FLMs behave in ways which stimulate and encourage this kind of behaviour.

Even in the most standardised organisation managers have some discretion over how they deliver HR policies. For example, the manager who carries out performance appraisals regularly (both formal and informally) in a way that is perceived to be fair and competent, and who provides an opportunity for feedback, is more likely to motivate his or her staff. Unlike the manager who just appraises people 'by the book' prompting employees to reciprocate with similar behaviour.

We look at how FLMs are themselves managed in, chapter four.

In this chapter we examine in more detail the relationship between FLMs and performance by providing further evidence of the link between employees' perceptions of management behaviour (in terms of how they carry out their people management role) and employee attitudinal and behavioural outcomes such as job satisfaction, motivation, commitment and job discretion. We ask does the way FLMs implement and enact HR policies by 'bringing them to life' and show leadership make a difference to the employees in their charge?

What do employees think of front line management?

To assess employee attitudes towards FLMs in terms of how well employees thought they carried out their people management role we used five questions rating how good managers were at:

- keeping everyone up to date about proposed changes

- providing everyone with the chance to comment on proposed changes

- responding to suggestions from employees

- dealing with problems at the workplace

- treating employees fairly.

See Figure 2.

Figure 2 | What employees think of front line managers' leadership activities

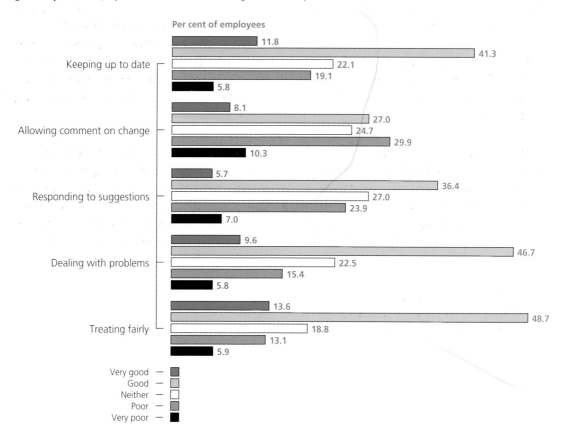

Taking as our sample all employees who were interviewed once over the two years (n = 608) we can see that FLMs were best at treating employees fairly (62 per cent felt that managers were 'good' or 'very good'), and worst at providing employees with a chance to comment on proposed changes (just over 40 per cent felt that managers were 'poor' or 'very poor' at this activity). However, these figures compare favourably with the Workplace Employee Relations Survey (WERS) data[1] – employees in our sample rated managers as better on all accounts than employees rated them in the WERS sample. We would expect this, however, if our previous analysis and assertions are correct, since these organisations were selected because they were known for their quality of HRM or were actively seeking to improve the link between people management and performance.

Yet there were significant variations across a range of employee characteristics – namely: occupation, age, length of service, length of time in the job, and hours worked.

◘ FLMs were more likely to rate their managers as being 'good' than professionals were, or workers were. For example, 73 per cent of FLMs felt their manager to be 'good'/'very good' at treating employees fairly, compared to 54 per cent of workers and 65 per cent of professionals.

◘ Older workers rated their managers as less good than younger workers. Only a quarter of employees aged 50 and over felt managers were 'good' at responding to suggestions from employees, compared to 44 per cent of those under 50 years old.

◘ The longer employees had been in the company and the job, the more likely they were to rate managers as 'poor'. Nearly half (48 per cent) of employees who had been in their job for five years or more felt that managers were 'poor' at providing everyone with a chance to comment on proposed changes, compared to 36 per cent of employees who had been in the job for less than a year.

◘ Employees working overtime/extra hours were more likely to rate their managers as 'good'/ 'very good' compared to those who did not work overtime. 50 per cent of employees who did not work extra hours rated their managers as 'poor'/'very poor' in providing them with a chance to comment on proposed changes, compared to 36 per cent of those who worked overtime.

There is therefore a discernible hierarchical pattern implying that non-managers rate their managers as less good than managers, and a clear association with age and length of service both in the organisation and the job such that older and longer-serving employees are more likely to rate managers as poor.

> *'... disillusion with management and cynicism is likely to set in the older the employee and the longer he or she has worked in the organisation.'*

This suggests that disillusion with management and cynicism is likely to set in the older the employee and the longer he or she has worked in the organisation.

The finding relating to overtime is interesting, suggesting that perhaps employees are grateful to their manager for providing them with the opportunity to work extra hours (when they are paid overtime) or have greater opportunity for contact with the manager and therefore more chance of being consulted, since they are liable to discuss why overtime is needed.

The relationship between attitudes towards front line managers and commitment, satisfaction, motivation and discretion

In order to explore the relationship between employee attitudes towards FLMs in their role in people management and employee attitudinal outcomes we combined the five variables mentioned above to make one composite variable (see Appendix 2), which we refer to as 'Relationship with FLM'.

Table 1 shows clearly that there is a strong association between those employees who felt that their managers were good at people management and their feelings toward their employer (commitment), the satisfaction they get from their job, their motivation and the extent to which they are given freedom to do their job or

have discretion and choice over how it is done. As one employee said:

My motivation and satisfaction varies from job to job, depending on the client and the manager and, crucially, how much influence I have over my job.

We can then do more sophisticated analysis to see if the way that managers behave actually influences employee attitudes and behaviours. Using multiple regression analysis we find that the factor 'Relationship with FLM' is the most important factor from our AMO model (see Figure 1, Chapter 1) in explaining the variation in job satisfaction and job discretion, and one of the most important in developing organisational commitment.

In other words, the higher the employees rate FLMs in terms of the way they manage people, the more committed and satisfied those employees will be, and the higher their levels of job discretion

Table 1 | Correlations between 'Relationship with FLM' and employee outcomes by company

Employee outcomes[2]	'Relationship with FLM'
Commitment	0.417**
Job satisfaction	0.524**
Motivation	0.360**
Job discretion	0.278**

** significant at the 0.01 level (2 tailed)

(and the lower they rate them, the less the commitment, satisfaction and discretionary behaviour).

For a greater understanding of this relationship we have looked at differences between organisations (Table 2).

It is evident that all companies showed a significant correlation or association between 'Relationship with FLM' and at least one employee attitudinal outcome (commitment, motivation, job satisfaction), and in all but one organisation there was a link with two employee attitude

outcomes. The relationships with commitment, job satisfaction and motivation were considered more fully in our earlier report (Purcell *et al*, 2003).

> *'... the higher the employees rate FLMs in terms of the way they manage people, the more committed and satisfied those employees will be, and the higher their levels of job discretion ...'*

The widespread results give us confidence in asserting that in all types of organisations the way FLMs undertake their people management roles plays a significant part in influencing employees' attitudes toward their organisation and their job.

Table 2 | The association between 'Relationship with FLM' and employee attitudinal outcomes by company

Company	Commitment	Job satisfaction	Motivation	Job discretion
Ait (38)	0.333**	0.354**		
Clerical Medical (38)		0.672**	0.446**	0.432**
Contact (55)	0.429**	0.336*		
Jaguar (61)	0.445**	0.613**	0.315**	0.316**
Nationwide (61)	0.435**	0.554**	0.382**	
OMT (45)	0.672**	0.436**	0.502**	
PWC (52)	0.305**	0.318*		
Royal Mint (58)		0.43**	0.281*	0.337**
RUH (54)	0.323*	0.493**	0.353**	
Selfridges (61)	0.448**	0.718**	0.569**	0.317*
Siemens (27)[3]			0.428*	
Tesco (58)	0.391**	0.554**	0.376**	
All (n = 608)	0.417**	0.524**	0.360**	0.28**

** correlations are significant at the 0.01 level (2 tailed)
* correlations are significant at the 0.05 level (2 tailed)

Discretionary behaviour

In four organisations there was a strong association between job discretion and 'Relationship with FLM' – the Royal Mint, Selfridges, Clerical Medical and Jaguar. 'Job discretion' in our survey referred to the amount of influence a person had over his or her job, and part of the explanation for this relationship can be found in the behaviour of FLMs.

The opportunity to engage in discretionary behaviour is crucial if employees are to perform well. At the Royal Mint teamworking and multi-skilling had been introduced two years prior to our interviews as part of a massive restructuring programme directed at introducing new working practices. Although all employees had undergone extensive training to multi-skill them, in practice the degree to which multi-skilling operated varied widely between shifts and depended largely on the behaviour of the team leader in terms of his or her willingness to allow multi-skilling to take place.

It also depended on the attitude of employees working on the shop floor. On one shift, in particular, where there was strong resistance to change, the team leader rather than embrace multi-skilling and allowed employees to retain their traditional methods of working.

At Selfridges, where individuality is highly regarded, team leaders encourage sales associates to use their discretion in terms of the way they handle the customers. At Jaguar, on the other hand, group leaders hold regular discussions with their teams on quality and work issues giving advice on how to do a task.

We are not saying that levels of job discretion were necessarily the highest in these organisations but that a strong association exists in these four organisations between the way FLMs exercise their people management role (as perceived by employees) and the influence employees have over their job. Part of the explanation for this, as we suggested earlier, is that employees' attitudes and therefore discretion are influenced by the way FLMs behave in delivering people management practices.

Levels of job discretion varied widely between organisations, and according to certain employee characteristics, such as occupation, length of service, and hours of work. FLMs themselves displayed higher levels of discretion than professionals and workers on the shop floor. Employees who had been with the organisation longer (and therefore were more experienced), full-timers and those who worked overtime also showed higher levels of influence over their jobs.

When we looked at differences between organisations, it was financial consultants (FCs) at Nationwide and staff at the small software company ait who displayed the highest levels of influence over their job.

At Nationwide, FC tend to work independently and are responsible for the hours they work (they maintain control over their diary), where they work (the majority are 'mobile', which means they cover a number of branches), and which customers or 'leads' to follow up. As one FCs explained:

My role is very independent within the Nationwide. I control both business and time management on a daily basis.

In other respects, however, there was less opportunity for flexibility because some of the work was governed by the financial services regulating body, particularly in terms of training requirements and the procedures that had to be followed. One might therefore expect the role of the FLMs (in this case senior financial consultants) to be more constrained or limited in this respect and have less of an impact on FCs. Yet when we compared all organisations in terms of 'Relationship with FLM', it was employees at Nationwide who rated their managers most highly.

One explanation for this is that because the FCs were responsible for their day-to-day work and required little day-to-day supervision, FLMs had more time to devote to their people management activities, such as involvement and communication, coaching and guidance.

A similar situation existed at ait. Employees enjoyed high levels of job autonomy – as one employee said:

I like the way we can organise the working day around what we want to do. You can manage your own time with no one looking over your shoulder

– and rated managers highly in comparison with other organisations. And yet there is no obvious statistical association between the two. The high levels of discretion are explained by the nature of the jobs being carried out. These were IT professionals (such as testers, database analysts and software developers) concerned with the application of knowledge, expertise and experience to solve often new and certainly challenging problems. Although they worked in project teams they were highly independent, requiring little traditional day-to-day management by the line manager, in this case the project manager.

Nevertheless the role of FLM was important in terms of communicating, involving, and developing employees (a key issue in the company), and this aspect of people management was highly regarded (see also Chapter 4).

Teamworking

Front line managers can also have a considerable impact on employee discretion in terms of the role they play in managing teams. In our survey we used two measures for teamworking:

◻ 'How would you describe the sense of teamworking in each of your work groups?'

and

◻ 'How effective do you think teamworking is in encouraging you to improve performance?'

Our data in Table 3 shows there to be a strong positive association between the sense of teamworking and job discretion, and between 'Relationship with FLM' and teamworking.

'Our research [shows] strong links between employees' views of FLMs' behaviour ... and performance.'

The relationship between teamworking and discretion or job autonomy is complex (Geary and Dobbins, 2001). Some studies provide positive accounts of teamworking and show that teams enhance employee discretion, which in turn impacts positively on employee job satisfaction, motivation and commitment (Pil and McDuffie, 1996).Other studies, however, take a more critical stance and claim that teamworking results in increased work intensification and stress because of increased management control, and this serves to undermine employee discretion.

Although a whole range of contextual factors can affect the impact of teamworking, it is clear that FLM behaviour is critical because poor management can undermine employee discretion and have a negative impact on team members. We need to do much further analysis to understand these relationships.

The link between front line management and performance

Our research does, however, show strong links between employees' views of FLMs' behaviour in the way they exercise their people management role and performance.

At Tesco we researched section managers (a first line management position) in four stores (in similar demographic areas), and it was apparent that variations in employee attitudes and behaviour, including discretion, were explained by differences in management behaviour. Tesco is a highly centralised organisation with standardised

Table 3 | Correlations between teamworking, job discretion and 'Relationship with FLM'

Employee outcomes	Sense of teamworking	Effectiveness of teamworking
'Relationship with FLM'	0.143**	0.232**
Job discretion	0.093*	0.112**

*** correlations are significant at the 0.01 level (2 tailed)*
** correlations are significant at the 0.05 level (2 tailed)*

policies, procedures and processes, and each store is governed by the company routine handbook which provides detailed information on how every task is to be performed. This in turn provides a guide to management behaviour.

In such an organisation we would therefore expect to find little variation in the delivery of managerial discretion between stores. Yet, as Table 4 shows, there were considerable variations in terms of employee job influence and employee views of management behaviour. (In this case the 'managers' are the senior management in the store, including the store manager.)

At Store C levels of influence over the job are clearly below those in other stores, only 27 per cent of employees saying they had a lot of influence over their job compared to 64 per cent in Store A. Employees' perceptions of management's role in people management are also lowest in

this store, only 18 per cent of employees feeling that their managers were 'good'/'very good' at responding to suggestions, compared to 82 per cent in Store B. Employee commitment to the organisation is also lowest in this store.

This data suggests that Store C had a very controlling style of management at the time of our interviews – a management that might well be described, for example, as poor at listening to and consulting staff. Significantly, when we looked at the performance indicators, Store C was the worst performer. So although there is heavy standardisation of routines, local senior managers are clearly able to exercise discretion in how they put policies into practice which may have an impact on performance. As one store manager remarked:

Store managers have to interpret what Head Office wants. Effectively, the store management is

Table 4 | Tesco: Four stores compared in terms of leadership, job influence and commitment (n=43)

Variable	Percentage of respondents in			
	Store A	Store B	Store C	Store D
Amount of influence over how job is done (% 'a lot')	64	64	27	50
How good are managers at (% 'good'/'very good'):				
– providing everyone with a chance to comment on changes?	53	72	18	30
– responding to suggestions?	27	82	18	60
– dealing with problems at the workplace?	73	82	55	70
Commitment (% 'proud to tell people' who they worked for)	91	73	46	90

the interface between Head Office and those who work in the store. The key is how you apply the Head Office policies – that's the difference!

I'm satisfied with the amount of influence I have over my job. My current team leader is good at listening to views and will take them up higher, and staff attitude survey results are discussed – I can feed my opinions up to higher mananagment.

Further evidence of the impact of FLMs on their team members came from three organisations which focused on changing the behaviour and attitudes of their FLMs. This resulted in significant improvements in employees' views of the way these managers handled people management, and this was also reflected in more positive employee attitudes and behaviours, and performance.

'A measurable outcome of this was improved staff retention ...'

In Chapter 4 we explore how these firms improved the way they managed their FLMs. Here we give examples of the outcome of these changes.

At the RUH, marked changes in employee attitudes took place in the second year of our research despite the hospital experiencing exceptional difficulties and adverse publicity in the local and national press. Much of this change could be attributed to deliberate attempts to improve line management, particularly at ward level. This came in the form of new recruitment and selection procedures for team leaders, emphasising people

management skills in addition to clinical skills, and introducing greater support and training for FLMs and a new appraisal scheme.

Job satisfaction, motivation and commitment all improved considerably. Levels of job discretion also improved slightly, 74 per cent claiming to have 'a lot' or 'some' influence over their job in year 1, compared to 82 per cent in year 2. And staff satisfaction with the amount of influence they had over how they did their job rose from 45 per cent to 61 per cent. As one employee said:

I'm very satisfied with my influence over my job. We've a new ward manager now. She's very approachable, a good listener, and gets to learn a lot. And people go to her – she's very supportive.

A measurable outcome of this was improved staff retention – a vital factor in nursing – as the level of vacancies fell from 11 (out of 32 posts) to none in year 2.

At Selfridges a similar pattern of changes in employee attitudes was observed. After our first-year interviews, the Manchester store that was the focus of our study took radical but positive steps to improve front line leadership (as described in Chapter 4).

Team leaders were asked to re-apply for their jobs using a new selection process which focused on behaviours as well as skill sets. This involved a half-day assessment including group exercises, interviews and role playing. Emphasis was placed on how these potential team leaders identified with others and connected with their team, and particular attention was placed on body language and verbal communication skills. The greater emphasis on the team leader role together with other changes in aspects of HR policy and practice (see Chapter 3) resulted in staff reporting better relationships with FLMs.

At the same time overall employee attitudes improved in terms of job satisfaction, motivation and commitment. Levels of employee discretion also improved, 56 per cent claiming to have 'a lot' of influence over their job the second year, compared to just 35 per cent in year 1. And levels of satisfaction with influence improved from 67 per cent to 73 per cent.

Performance also improved in the store, and at the end of our second year of study, sales were up 23 per cent compared to the previous year. Contribution – the difference between revenue and cost – was particularly impressive. In our main unit of analysis (ladies' wear, where many of the changes took effect) they reported the best record of labour turnover and the second best absence rate (4.9 per cent).

Since our research formally ended at the store, Selfridges have continued to focus on front line management, re-defining the role in 2002 by issuing team leader 'role guides' in order to give greater clarity to the role and greater emphasis to the people management aspects (for more detail, see page 8). All team leaders went through

eight days of training in 2002, covering mainly aspects of people management such as discipline, recruitment and selection, and training, coaching and development.

Again a similar picture emerged at Clerical Medical, where a new manager in charge of one part of our unit of analysis wanted to introduce more team-based involvement, improve the operation of the appraisal scheme, and generally enhance brand awareness and efficiency through a initiative called 'Living the brand'. Changes also took place at team leader level, with a much greater emphasis being placed on people management skills.

Attitudes towards managers improved in the second year, as did levels of commitment, job satisfaction and motivation. Employees also reported higher levels of discretion (68 per cent claimed to have 'a lot' of influence in year 2, compared to 30 per cent in year 1), and more satisfaction with their levels of influence (rising from 70 per cent to 88 per cent). As two employees said:

I'm more satisfied now … I have a new boss who lets me get on with my job. I'm trusted again.

The job is changing all the time, and Clerical Medical do recognise that we are important and are giving us more influence.

As with the other two cases reported here, performance at Clerical Medical improved in the second year of our research as market share increased.

Summary

In this chapter we have explored the relationship between FLMs and performance, and shown that the way in which FLMs implement and enact HR policies by 'bringing them to life' and show leadership plays a significant part in influencing employees' attitudes towards the organisation and their jobs. Indeed, FLM behaviour is the most important factor from our model in explaining the variation in both job satisfaction and job discretion or the choice people have over how to do their jobs. It is also one of the most important factors in developing organisational commitment.

We focused on discretionary behaviour and saw how in four organisations in particular the amount of influence people have over their jobs was influenced by the way FLMs deliver people management practices. FLMs also have a critical role to play in managing teams – poor management behaviour can undermine team members' discretion. Finally, we showed how in some organisations it was possible to demonstrate a link between the way FLMs undertake their people management roles and organisational performance.

Endnotes

1   The workplace Employee Relations Survey (WERS) 1998 is based on large samples which are representative of the great majority of workplaces in Great Britain and involves interviews with managers, employee representatives and employees.

2   Commitment is a combination of three questions, as is job satisfaction. Job influence is a single question – see Appendix 1.

3   Data for Siemens was collected only in the first year of this survey.

Chapter 3

◘ **Explores how front line managers deliver people management activities**

◘ **Examines the gap between formal policy and actual practice**

3 | Where do front line managers make a difference?

Introduction

We know from surveys that over the last decade front line managers have played a more prominent role in people management activities as an increasing number of HR practices have been devolved to them. In the mid-1990s, for example, Hutchinson and Wood (1995) reported greater line manager involvement in personnel issues such as recruitment, training and disciplinary decisions compared to five years earlier. This devolution was often accompanied by decentralisation within organisations, sometimes due to privatisation or deregulation. The 1998 WERS survey (Cully *et al*, 1999) found that supervisors were more likely to play a part in HR-type decisions than they previously had, nine out of ten workplace managers claiming primary responsibility for employee relations matters, and spending on average 35 per cent of their time on them.

In support of this trend it is argued that HR policies should be 'owned' by the line rather than being held by a specialist function (Guest, 1991) because it is these managers who are directly responsible for supervising staff on a daily basis and who are ultimately responsible for their performance. There can be other benefits too, such as reduced costs and speedier decision-making (Larsen and Brewster, 2000).

However, line manager involvement in these activities is not without its difficulties. For example, line managers may not want this responsibility, may not have the time or authority to deal with it, or may lack the ability to handle these issues effectively (Larsen and Brewster, 2000; Renwick, 2002).

In this chapter we explore the impact of front line managers on the delivery of these people management activities in more detail. Our research shows there to be a strong relationship between employee perceptions of FLM behaviour and the following HR activities/concerns: involvement, communication, teamworking, work–life balance, rewards, training, performance appraisal, career opportunities, job security and 'openness' (see Table 5).

Further analysis, based on comparisons between year 1 and year 2 data sets, suggests that an improvement in front line management behaviour is associated with an improvement in these practices in terms of satisfaction with pay, training and development, a better sense of teamworking, and so on. Here we focus on a number of key areas in which managers have considerable involvement and make a difference:

> *'Performance appraisal is an area in which front line managers have [a] key role ... to play in the delivery of HR policies.'*

- performance appraisal

- training, coaching and guidance

- involvement and communication

- 'openness', or the ability to express grievances and raise concerns

Table 5 | Correlations between 'relationship with FLM' and HR activities

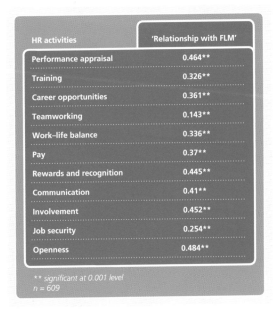

HR activities	'Relationship with FLM'
Performance appraisal	0.464**
Training	0.326**
Career opportunities	0.361**
Teamworking	0.143**
Work–life balance	0.336**
Pay	0.37**
Rewards and recognition	0.445**
Communication	0.41**
Involvement	0.452**
Job security	0.254**
Openness	0.484**

** significant at 0.001 level
n = 609

- work–life balance

- recognition.

The role of front line managers in managing teams has been dealt with separately in Chapter 1.

Performance appraisal

Performance appraisal is an area in which front line managers have traditionally had direct involvement with their staff, and provides a good example of the key role these managers have to play in the delivery of HR policies.

Appraisal is important not only as a means of directly managing individual performance but as a tool to reinforce corporate values and help maintain employee loyalty and commitment. It also clearly links with other HR practices such as pay, training, career development, and communication. Nevertheless, as the wide body of literature on the subject acknowledges, the performance appraisal process contains considerable difficulties for both employees and managers (Redman, 2001; Grint, 1993) and is ranked as the 'most disliked managerial activity' (Carroll and Schneier, 1982).

Here we consider the practice of performance appraisal in our case study organisations, emphasising the role that managers have to play by examining the differences between company policy and practice, difficulties with appraisals schemes, and trends in selected organisations.

All but the two manufacturing organisations (Jaguar and Royal Mint) operated a formal performance appraisal system for all employees interviewed, although the type of system varied considerably. In all organisations front line managers played a key role in the appraisal process, and in the majority of cases (Clerical Medial, Contact 24, Nationwide, OMT, Selfridges, Siemens, Tesco) the appraisal was conducted by the immediate line manager and usually involved the appraisee/employee and manager jointly reviewing progress and future objectives. At ait, where there was no traditional line manager role, the appraisal review was shared between professional leaders (senior staff) who dealt with the developmental aspect and project

managers who handled the reward element. Two other organisations – the RUH (see box on page 30) and PWC – involved multi-raters in the feedback process, although it was a manager who conducted the main appraisal interview. At PWC, for example, feedback was obtained after each assignment from team members, including the project manager, plus the client through a customer satisfaction survey. This information was collated and fed into the annual performance review which was conducted by a 'counselling manager', a senior manager, who then graded individual performance.

Company policy on the frequency of formal appraisals also varied, five organisations claiming

Table 6 | The frequency of formal performance appraisals, as reported by employees by company – based on Year 2 data (percentage of employees)

Company (n)	Never/Not in the last year	Once a year	Twice a year	Three times a year	Quarterly	Other
Ait (33)	3	61	33		3	
Clerical Medical (34)	3	6	3	23	65	
Contact 24 (40)	13	27	38	17	5	
Nationwide (49)		25	26		47	2
OMT (39)		91	7		2	
PWC (27)		26	63		4	7
RUH (38)	18*	74	8			
Selfridges (41)	10	7	76	2	2	2
Siemens (27) (Yr1)		83	13			
Tesco (39)	21	31	18	3	28	

* This was a new performance appraisal system, and the first appraisal was being undertaken during the time of our second year interviews. Some staff were therefore still waiting for their appraisal.

to have annual appraisals, three twice a year, one three times a year, and one four times a year. However, as Table 6 shows, the frequency of performance appraisals, as reported by employees, varied not only between the case studies but more significantly within each organisation. In other words, there was a clear discrepancy between the practice and the policy in all organisations, suggesting variations between managers within the same organisation.

This gap between policy and practice is further exposed when we consider the purpose of the appraisal scheme. In all organisations the stated aim of the appraisal scheme was developmental, and in six organisations it was also linked to some form of reward. However, employees' views on the purpose of the appraisal scheme again differed from company policy (Table 7).

Looking at the sample of all employees interviewed over the two years (n = 608) we find that performance appraisal was rated as the least effective HR policy (in terms of levels of satisfaction) after pay, and in a fair number of organisations it was the least favourite HR activity. The reasons given were numerous, and included the views that the measurements and targets were felt to be unclear and/or not relevant, and that the system was too complicated or time-consuming. Many of the problems could be directly linked to the behaviour of managers, as the interviews with employees revealed:

Table 7 | The purpose of the performance appraisal scheme, as reported by employees by company – based on Year 2 data (percentage of employees)

Company (n)	Pay	Training and development	Both	Don't know
Ait (33)	19	3	78	
Clerical Medical (34)	6	32	62	
Contact 24 (40)	6	52	34	8
Nationwide (49)	14		86	
OMT (39)		58	33	9
PWC (27)	27	8	65	
RUH (38)		88	3	9
Selfridges (41)		19	78	3
Siemens (27) (Yr 1)	7	37	56	
Tesco (39)	3	90	5	3

Managers are not good at talking to you about performance …

The ideas are good but the execution is not – it's rushed through at the year end.

Your appraisal depends on who is doing the appraisal.

It seems rather subjective … There are concerns that if you've got problems and you raise them, you're perceived as being negative – although it does vary from one line manager to the next.

I'd like to see more consistency from professional leaders – more discussion and understanding about performance.

The pay aspect is down to line manager discretion rather than based on actual information. It depends on how well you get on with your line manager …

The interviews revealed that some managers were not considered good at providing feedback, or rushed through the appraisal meeting giving little time for discussion, or were reluctant to deal with poor performers. And in organisations where appraisal was linked to pay, some employees felt that managers manipulated the results. One of the most commonly cited reasons for dissatisfaction, however, concerned the frequency of appraisals and the fact that reviews were either simply not taking place or not taking place as often as they should.

Appraisal is not happening. Monitoring has gone by the wayside at the moment. They expect too much of team leaders – it changed a few years ago, and they are bogged down in stats …

If appraisals were done regularly and we got feedback, I'm sure performance would increase …

Another very common complaint was that the process was subjective, particularly when competency or behavioural measurements were used, making the system vulnerable to inconsistent treatment by managers.

> **'One of the most commonly cited reasons for dissatisfaction [was] that reviews were either simply not taking place or not taking place as often as they should.'**

Interestingly, financial consultants at the Nationwide displayed the highest levels of satisfaction with their appraisal scheme in year 1, possibly because it was the only scheme that used 100-per-cent objective-based measures which were clear and not subject to differing interpretations by line managers and employees. In the second year, however, levels of satisfaction with the appraisal scheme fell when an element of subjectivity was introduced through the use of behavioural objectives. As one financial consultant remarked:

The behaviours aspect is too subjective and can depend on your relationship with the line manager

… The behaviours side takes an element of fairness out of the system.

Why are managers not necessarily good at carrying out and conducting performance appraisals (despite the fact that, according to research, they think they are good!)? According to the literature (Redman, 2001), many managers lack the necessary skills and training, or dislike the bureaucracy involved (Harris, 2001), leading to 'abdication management' and an unwillingness to accept responsibility for decisions made, or perceive the practice as not adding value to the organisation. Lawler (1994: 17), for example, suggests that it is an 'unnatural act' for managers, with the result that if they are not trained properly, it is done poorly.

Managers also play organisational games with performance ratings (Snape *et al*, 1994), for example inflating ratings in the hope that good appraisals will reflect favourably on themselves.

Three organisations made changes to their appraisal scheme during the course of our research, and provide further evidence on the impact of managers. At both the RUH and Selfridges changes were made after our first-year interviews to improve front line leadership coupled with improvements to the appraisal scheme, resulting in improved levels of satisfaction with the appraisal scheme (see boxes).

A similar pattern of results emerged at Clerical Medical, where improvements were made to both team leader roles and the appraisal scheme. The frequency of appraisals was reduced and a new form of measurement introduced which resulted in levels of satisfaction with the appraisal scheme increasing from 30 per cent in year 1 to 50 per cent in year 2.

RUH

In the second year of our research, the RUH introduced a new system of 360-degree feedback whereby each employee nominates four or five colleagues to appraise him or her. The colleagues are from any grade, although they ideally include a person on the same grade, one above and one below. Evaluation is based on teamwork, communication, clinical skills, teaching and 'other comments'. These are sent to the line manager who provides feedback at an appraisal interview. Although time-consuming, the system has been welcomed by staff. Levels of satisfaction with the appraisal scheme rose from 55 per cent in year 1 to 74 per cent in year 2 As one nurse remarked:

It's useful to know what my peers think of me … and my line manager has the right skills for feedback.

<table>
<tr><td>

Selfridges

At the Trafford Centre store in Manchester formal performance appraisals are conducted twice a year, and until recently were used for both pay and training development purposes although the issues were dealt with separately (the March/April review dealing with the pay aspect, and the September/ October review with development). After feedback on the findings from our first year interviews, the store made changes to front line leadership (see Chapters 2 and 4) coupled with changes to the appraisal scheme, such as linking it more to succession planning. This ensured that the team leaders took greater ownership of the process, and as a result satisfaction with the appraisal scheme increased significantly, from 59 per cent in year 1 to 84 per cent in year 2. As one sales associate remarked:

We now have a manager who gets appraisals done ... and we get praise now, and little gifts – such as perfume.

Further changes were made in 2003, removing the link with pay, and the process is now referred to as the 'development review'. The view of team leaders who were subsequently interviewed was that this had further improved the scheme because, as one team leader remarked:

When it was linked to pay, people were not honest about their performance.

</td></tr>
</table>

Training, coaching and guidance

The formal performance appraisal process is just one means of involving managers in the development and performance of their staff. In addition to this, managers are increasingly expected to play a role in training and coaching staff both formally and informally.

In our survey 85 per cent of employees reported receiving some formal training over the previous 12 months, and 58 per cent had received one week or more of training over the previous year. Nearly half said this was off-the-job training, 20 per cent on-the-job training, and 29 per cent said it was a combination. Assuming that the majority of off-the-job training is provided by a training specialist (Selfridges and Contact 24 have specialist team trainers, for example), this suggests that a substantial amount of formal training was provided on the job, which in most cases would be by the line manager.

In addition to this, there is often on going informal training and coaching from the line manager, as these team leaders explain:

I show people how to do the job. I encourage questions and provide as much training as required ...

I'm here all the time. I put information on file for them to read, and I stand back and observe, and then help them with problems.

We were able to explore FLM involvement in this HR activity further by asking the question:

☐ 'To what extent does your line manager provide you with coaching and guidance to improve your performance?'

The results for all employees (n = 609) are shown below (Figure 3).

Considerable variations were shown between organisations, however. Employees at Nationwide felt their line managers to be most effective (in year 1, for example, 50 per cent felt their line manager helped them 'to a great extent', 39 per cent 'to some extent', and only 11 per cent 'to a limited extent'). This is partly because these employees, financial consultants (FCs), operated in a highly regulated environment (qualified FCs

Figure 3 | The provision of coaching and/or guidance by front line managers

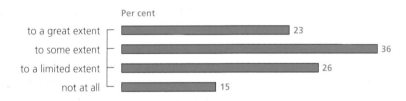

Figure 4 | Differences between occupational groups in the provision of coaching and guidance (N608)
To what extent does your line manager provide you with coaching and guidance to improve your performance?

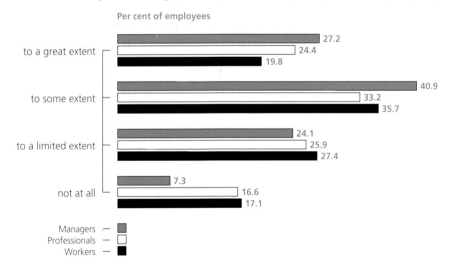

were expected to have 50 hours of CPD training), and senior financial consultants (the line manager) were required to meet FCs once a month for training and communication purposes (for a trainee this could be weekly).

Interestingly, compared to the other case study organisations, these employees were also the most satisfied in terms of their level of training (84 per cent were satisfied) and exhibited the highest levels of commitment, job satisfaction and motivation.

Intriguing differences were also found between occupations (see Figure 4), age, and length of service in the job – managers, young people and those with a short length of service being more likely to rate their manager as more effective in terms of helping them to improve performance.

- 25 per cent of employees over the age of 50 felt that their manager did not help them at all, compared to just 9 per cent of those under 29.

- 27 per cent of employees who had been in the job for less than two years felt that managers helped them to 'a great extent', compared to 14 per cent who had been in the job five years or more.

- Just 7 per cent of managers said their line manager did not help them at all with coaching or guidance, compared to 17 per cent of workers and 17 per cent of professionals.

We would expect to find differences according to length of service in the job and possibly age, because the longer a person is in the job, the more experienced he or she becomes and the less the need for help from the line manager.

Table 8 | Correlations with the provision of coaching and guidance by the line manager

	Provision of coaching and guidance by manager to improve performance
Satisfaction with training	0.309**
Satisfaction with career opportunities	0.266**
Satisfaction with performance appraisal	0.337**
Sense of teamworking	0.114**
Commitment	0.197**
Job satisfaction	0.361**
Motivation	0.248**

** significant at 0.01 level (2 tailed)

RUH

At the RUH, improvements in front line management plus the new appraisal system resulted in a much greater emphasis on training and development. Nurses, for example, were now allowed to go on pre-booked courses rather than cancelling them at the last minute because of staff shortages, as had previously been the practice. Staff were encouraged to move on, and the new performance appraisal scheme ensured that appraisals were performed in a constructive fashion. In year 2 nearly 90 per cent said they had discussed their training and development needs with their line managers over the previous 12 months, compared to 64 per cent in year 1, and nearly three quarters felt that their line managers had helped them with coaching and guidance to either a 'great extent' or 'some extent', compared to 51 per cent the previous year. Consequently, both satisfaction with training and career opportunities rose significantly (from 54 per cent to 87 per cent).

Selfridges

Shortly after our second-year interviews at Selfridges the role of team leaders was redefined with a much greater emphasis on people management activities (see Chapters 1 and 2), including 'coaching and counselling'. The coaching role involves observing around five sales associates (out of a team which can be as large as 26 full-time and part-time staff) each week and providing instant feedback rather that waiting for the formal development review. If the observation of one person proves unfavourable, the individual concerned is observed again the following week; if favourable, the individual receives a file recording positive behaviour. Combined with this role is that of 'counsellor' whereby team leaders monitor staff on absence, sickness, lateness, attitude and conduct on a monthly basis. This can form a substantial part of the job, depending on which department is involved. For example, menswear was a particularly problematic area because, according to the team leader who had recently moved to this department from ladieswear,

Women care – they call in and phone, if they are off sick. But lads don't even phone. This makes managing absence harder.

Team leaders can discipline staff up to the first level of written warning.

Further analysis highlights the importance of managers in the delivery of training, coaching and guidance in a number of ways. Firstly, there is a strong correlation or relationship between the effective provision of coaching and guidance by the line manager and levels of satisfaction with training, career opportunities, performance appraisal, sense of teamworking, commitment, satisfaction and motivation (see Table 8). In other words, the better the coaching and guidance provided by the line manager, the more likely employees are to be satisfied with their training, appraisal, career opportunities and job, the better the sense of teamworking, and the more committed and motivated employees are likely to be.

Secondly, three organisations – the RUH, Selfridges and Clerical Medical – showed significant improvements over the two-year period of study in terms of the provision of coaching and guidance by line managers, which were reflected in improved levels of satisfaction with both training and career opportunities (see boxes).

Involvement and communication

Employee involvement practices (we include communication practices in this) can have a positive effect on employees' attitudes such as job satisfaction and commitment and ultimately on performance. However, according to research (Marchington, 2001; Fenton O'Creevy, 2001), many of these initiatives fail to become established or do not produce the desired effects because

of management actions – or inactions. For example, in his analysis of employee involvement Marchington (2001; p.238) shows that there are often

significant gaps between formal policy statements and senior management beliefs and assumptions on the one hand, and the reality of employee involvement at workplace level,

and that this can be partly attributed to the line manager. He suggests that employee involvement schemes sometimes fail in the conversion of policy into practice because line managers may not be committed to them, may not have the ability needed to make the schemes work well, may be doubtful about the value of employee involvement schemes, may lack training on how to operate such schemes, or may simply suffer from work overload and lack the time to communicate or consult.

This belief that there is a policy–practice gap and that line managers may be a barrier to the success of employee involvement initiatives also holds true for the organisations in our study.

> *'... firstly, not all staff were aware of the existence of these initiatives, and ... secondly, an even lower proportion of employees claimed to have been practically concerned in such schemes.'*

Table 9 shows those organisations which claimed to have formal employee involvement schemes (excluding teamworking) for *all* their employees, and the variety of schemes that existed. Significantly, the table shows that firstly, not all staff were aware of the existence of these initiatives, and that secondly, an even lower proportion of employees claimed to have been practically concerned in such schemes.

In one of our companies some employees spoke highly of the team briefing session where production, scheduling and quality problems were constructively discussed. Others, however, claimed to have no knowledge of such a scheme and no sense of involvement. When the interviewer checked up on team briefings, which were meant to happen each week, one worker replied,

Oh, you mean those sessions where we are told off and shouted at …

(although the language used was more colourful!). This shows clearly that involvement relies on the approach the FLM uses – much more than simple time allocation for a meeting activity.

An alternative measure of employee involvement is to consider the frequency of consultation on certain issues, and this would cover involvement through both formal and informal mechanisms. In our survey employees were asked how frequently they were consulted by managers for their views on five separate issues:

◘ future plans at the workplace

Table 9 | Policy and practice of employee involvement schemes (other than teamworking) in selected organisations

Company (n)	Examples of types of formal employee involvement schemes	Percentage of employees interviewed aware of employee involvement schemes	Percentage of employees interviewed practically concerned in employee involvement schemes
Ait (38)	T Group, vocational groups, 'brown bag' meetings	84	74
Clerical Medical (38)	Forums, project teams, focus groups	84	74
PWC (51)	Peer-group meetings, team talk, focus groups	76	53
Royal Mint (58)	Team briefing	76	63
RUH (54)	Ward meetings, unit meetings,	74	63
Selfridges (60)	Forum, daily briefs	55	30
Tesco (57)	Forums, team briefs, workshops	91	77

◻ staffing issues

◻ changes to work practices

◻ pay issues

◻ health and safety issues.

As Figure 5 shows, the overall level of participation in workplace decision-making appears to be low, the most widespread consultation being about changes to work practices and the least about pay issues.

It is interesting to compare this to the WERS data, which shows that health and safety issues received the most widespread consultation (23 per cent of employees reported frequent contact on this issue). This difference is most likely explained by the predominance of service sector organisations in our study for whom health and safety is seen as less critical.

Our own data also showed that consultation was greatest with managers, followed by professionals, and least among workers. This is not surprising in

Figure 5 | Consultation by front line managers (N608)

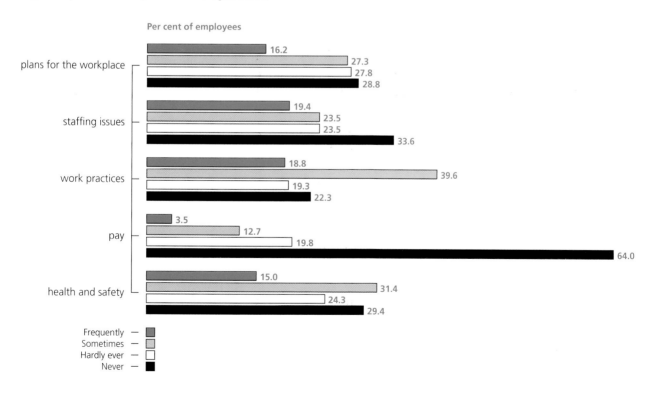

Per cent of employees

plans for the workplace
- 16.2
- 27.3
- 27.8
- 28.8

staffing issues
- 19.4
- 23.5
- 23.5
- 33.6

work practices
- 18.8
- 39.6
- 19.3
- 22.3

pay
- 3.5
- 12.7
- 19.8
- 64.0

health and safety
- 15.0
- 31.4
- 24.3
- 29.4

Frequently —
Sometimes —
Hardly ever —
Never —

that we might expect involvement to be greater higher up the hierarchical scale.

Employees were also asked to specify how good they thought managers were over three different dimensions of employee involvement and communication:

◘ keeping everyone up to date on proposed changes

◘ providing everyone with the chance to comment on proposed changes

◘ responding to suggestions from employees.

The results are shown in Figure 6.

Managers appeared best at keeping employees informed about proposed changes, but were less good at consulting them for their views or responding to suggestions from employees. A common complaint that ran through all organisations was that employees were not listened to by their managers, and that their views were ignored.

I have suggested things in the past – but I might as well sit in a corner and say nothing. The white coats always think they are right.

Figure 6 | How good are managers at involvement and participation?

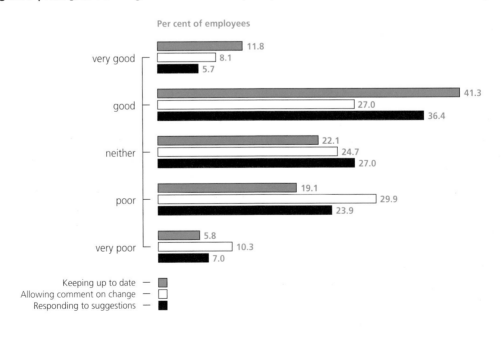

Per cent of employees

Keeping up to date
Allowing comment on change
Responding to suggestions

People who work on the job know it best. But we are the last to be asked. They should ask us how to improve, but they just implement.

We're not given any say in what's happening – if you don't like it, lump it. We can see other ways of doing things, but we're not listened to. It's what the powers-that-be say it will be.

If you're asked anything or suggest anything, it is not good, and you are told 'This is the way to do it.' If you ask the supervisor, you are told that you do not need to know – so you don't bother in the end.

Significant variations were found by occupation, age, length of service, and hours of work. Professionals, young people and those with a shorter length of service rated their managers more highly in terms of employee involvement and communication.

There were also variations between organisations, managers at ait (see box page 40) and Nationwide being perceived as best at providing support for employee participation in both years. This is particularly impressive at ait, which ran into difficulties shortly after the second year of our study as the share value of the company plummeted, forcing management to make redundancies.

In three organisations employees felt that managers had improved quite signifanctly over the two-year period of our research – Selfridges, RUH

and Clerical Medical – which can be attributed to the positive changes all three organisations had made in terms of leadership (as referred to earlier).

Communication on the ward is excellent now. Our manager is very approachable. She's in the coffee room with us, and so on …
(RUH)

I feel more satisfied with my job because we have a new team leader now … And we have more say, ward meetings are held every month, and issues are being addressed.
(RUH)

It has improved here over the last 12 months in communication – managers are more approachable now, and aware of what staff feel …
(Clerical Medical)

I feel satisfied with my level of involvement now because I have a good team leader who listens and gets things done.
(Selfridges)

However, despite improvements at Selfridges their 2002 staff survey identified communication as a key concern, particularly among part-time evening staff who missed out on the morning daily brief delivered by team leaders. Selfridges reacted to this by introducing a further two briefings in the day so that team leaders now have to provide three briefings during the day, at 09.45, 13.45 and 17.00.

Ait

Ait is built around series of communities which form a network for communication and involvement. The main means of communication is known as T-Groups – groups which are non-hierarchical and cross-functional, drawing together employees from all parts of the organisation including professional and non-professional staff. The leaders of these teams are trained and may occupy either senior or junior posts within the organisation. There are also vocational communities which provide a forum for specialists, such as testers or builders, to meet and discuss issues of common interest, and project or operational teams based around work for a particular client. In addition there are extensive knowledge-sharing activities across the organisation through the use of both formal means (such as the intranet) and informal schemes, such as 'brown bag' meetings, which are regular lunchtime briefings where staff may make presentations on projects they have been involved in. In the second year the T-Group was changed to allow for upward as well as downward communication. As one employee remarked:

There's a more dynamic feel to the T-Group system. There has been a change in emphasis and it's now more two-way – it's seen as more responsive.

Recognition

A key issue that is often neglected in studies which explore the connection between people management practices and performance is recognition, and here again front line managers have a pivotal role to play. By 'recognition' we mean the extent to which employees feel that their contribution and even their existence is recognised and respected by their line manager and the organisation generally.

Recognition can be a powerful motivator (see for example Maslow's [1943] work on the Hierarchy of needs), and a means of improving employee satisfaction and commitment. Employees like and need to know not only how well they are doing but also that their achievements are being acknowledged and appreciated – and this came across strongly in our interviews.

In all our case study organisations employees felt less satisfied with their rewards and recognition than they did with their pay and other benefits, suggesting that failure to offer sufficient recognition was the culprit. As one disgruntled employee remarked:

Recognition is non-existent – you're just a bum on a seat at times. It's only through team spirit that I stay here.

'Recognition can be a powerful motivator, and a means of improving employee satisfaction and commitment.'

When asked what other methods would improve their performance, the most common answer was 'recognition' – as the following remarks illustrate:

If someone comes down and says you are doing a good job or you handled that well, it is worth more than a good pay rise... and that's lacking now.

What would improve my performance? More talking to you, better appraisal, and saying 'Thank you' – appreciation.

Managers should take a closer look at people and give praise where it's due and tell people they are doing a good job.

Managers can show recognition by listening and responding to suggestions (addressed in the previous section), but also, as the above quotes suggest, by praising good work – by just saying a simple 'Thank you' or 'Well done.' Other actions might include offering tokens or prizes. At Selfridges small incentives were offered to staff who performed well, such as vouchers, cakes or bottles of wine, which were particularly helpful if, as this employee suggests, the team bonus was not going to be paid that month:

I know the targets – we sit down to daily targets. But we also have local bonuses for staff, like a bottle of wine or perfume, which keeps interest going, especially if the team bonus is not going to pay out.

At the Nationwide one of the most coveted awards for financial consultants was the monthly 'Diamond club' award, which was an award certificate (plus pin badge!) presented to top performers.

Openness

'Openness' or the ability to raise grievances and matters of concern was explored in our interviews by asking the question

◘ To what extent do you feel your company provides you with reasonable opportunities to express grievances and raise personal concerns?

Although this question refers to 'the company', increasingly front line managers are taking responsibility for these matters and, as was the case in all of our case study organisations, line managers were the first point of contact under the company grievances procedure. Line managers were also responsible for handling absence and sickness – for example, ringing up employees who did not turn up for work or conducting back-to-work interviews for absent staff – and under these circumstances were likely to hear about personal problems and concerns. If an employee wanted to change his or her hours of work for personal reasons, again it would be the line managers who would be contacted in the first instance, rather than the personnel or HR department.

'Our data shows there to be a significant positive relationship between management behaviour and the extent to which the company provides opportunities for people to express grievances and raise personal concerns.'

Our data (table 5, page 26) shows there to be a significant positive relationship between management behaviour and the extent to which the company provides opportunities for people to express grievances and raise personal concerns. Over 60 per cent of employees interviewed felt their company to be 'very effective' or 'quite effective' at openness, although again there were variations by organisation, Nationwide and Clerical Medical being perceived as being the most effective. There were also significant variations between occupations, with workers more likely to rate their organisation higher than professionals and managers.

Work–life balance

FLMs also have a key role to play in the delivery of work–life balance policies, by for example being flexible on hours of work or time off – as the following interviewee suggests:

Work–life balance attitudes are improving … I know which departments and managers I would go to for the family-friendly approach.

60 per cent of employees interviewed felt that their organisation was 'very good' (15 per cent) or 'quite good' (45 per cent) at helping employees

achieve a balance between home life and work. Surprisingly, there were no significant differences between males and females, although there were between full-time and part-time staff, occupation and number of overtime hours worked. Full-time employees, managers and those who worked long hours rated the organisation worse than part-timers and workers.

The commonest complaint, inevitably, related to hours of work either in terms of being too long or unsocial, or too inflexible. Last-minute roster changes were particularly resented:

The ridiculous hours and the constantly changing rotas at the drop of a hat makes it impossible to have a social life and difficult to get into home-life mode.

I have to spend a long time away from home – for example, 10 hours in Dorking. I had hobbies when I started here, but now I can't commit to them.

Recent research (Bond and Wise, 2003) also suggests that line managers' knowledge of both statutory and company family leave is often wanting owng to poor communication, training and support, leading to inconsistencies in the application of such policies.

Summary

In this chapter we have considered the impact of front line managers in the delivery of people management practices, focusing on their role in performance appraisal, training, coaching and guidance, involvement and communication, recognition, 'openness' and work–life balance.

Our research shows that FLMs were responsible for the implementation of these HR activities, and that there exists a strong relationship between employee perceptions of FLM behaviour and these practices. Further analysis suggests that an improvement in FLM behaviour is associated with an improvement in these practices, such as satisfaction with training, involvement and communication, and so on.

We have also seen a clear gap between formal policy statements and practice – in other words, between the rhetoric and the reality – and this concurs with previous research by Marchington (2001) and McGovern *et al* (1997).

The significance for this piece of research is that the difference can be partly attributed to front line management, for a whole raft of reasons. For example, they may suffer from work overload and not have the time, may not be committed to particular initiatives, may dislike the bureaucracy involved, may not wish to have responsibility for these matters, or may lack skills and training to perform them well. These issues are pursued in the next chapter of this report.

Chapter 4

◪ **Examines management strategies for front line managers themselves**

◪ **Discusses the nature of the relationship between front line managers and their managers and how this can impact on performance**

4 | Managing the managers

Introduction

We have shown in previous chapters how the way front line managers implement and enact HR policies and practices and show leadership in the 'doing' of management – communicating, involving, counselling, guiding and controlling – makes a real difference. We have discussed how the move to line management responsibility for the delivery of HRM added to the tendency to decentralise responsibilities down the line has increased the importance of FLMs.

As employment relations has become more individualised, focusing on the contribution each employee can make, so the job of FLMs has become richer – but also more stressful with competing priorities. Studies of line managers (eg Whittaker and Marchington, 2003) have shown that the devolution of HR responsibilities to the line has left many under-prepared, under-supported and under-trained, and crucially when faced with competing priorities, having to choose between conflicting goals.

One of our respondents referred to the difference between his management duties and his leadership role. The need to meet defined,

measurable targets directly related to prime performance and profitability standards can drive out the space and the inclination to engage in the so-called soft skills of leadership.

If the secret to linking people management to performance is to 'unlock' or trigger discretionary behaviour in employees in the way they do their job, work with others and take initiatives, the same is true for FLMs – in fact, it is probably more important, since it will impact on those they manage.

In many cases the exercising of the soft skills of leadership, and the application of these 'doing' HR practices is discretionary in the sense that it is hard to allocate time for these duties because they are part of daily management. Some argue that this is where line managers need to utilise their 'emotional intelligence' – another feature of discretionary behaviour.

It follows – indeed, it is obvious – that the way line managers are themselves managed will be likely to influence their discretionary behaviour positively or negatively. Although we did not focus on this in our study, and much more research is needed here, we were able to use our data to draw some important conclusions.

We also have the experience of a number of companies who tried to change the way FLMs were selected and put more emphasis on their leadership and 'doing' roles. We give some evidence of the outcome of these initiatives in this chapter.

> *'... we have been able to isolate those factors in the way managers are managed that really make a difference.'*

Line manager commitment and job satisfaction

We begin by looking at the results of the employee surveys we undertook in each company. Overall, we interviewed 165 managers or people who had some management and leadership responsibilities, especially in dealing directly with 'their' employees. Usually this was a team, and so job titles – as noted in Chapter 1 – often did not use the word 'manager', replacing it with 'leader' as in team leader or group leader.

The sample reported in this chapter covers the 12 People and Performance companies and the six much smaller companies in the knowledge intensive company research. In one case, Tesco, all of our sample of employees were line managers on the lowest tier of the managerial hierarchy, called section managers, each responsible for around 12 employees. In another, PWC, 28 of the 70 interviews we conducted were with managers, usually people who had just qualified as accountants and now had some team leadership responsibilities.

By using the whole sample and doing rather more sophisticated statistical analysis than we were able to do in the original report, we have been able to isolate those factors in the way managers are managed that really make a difference. Of course, these are general statements covering a wide range of different types of companies and very different types of products and services. A factor may be important in one company but not in another. Nevertheless, the overall position is indicative of what type of HR policies applied to line managers are likely to be effective if properly done.

One general observation is that our FLMs tended to have, or show, higher levels of commitment to their employer, satisfaction with their job and levels of motivation than other employees. In other words, as a group they are more predisposed to their company and their job than those they manage, and the benefits of good practice are more likely to flow from this.

Table 10 shows the statistically significant associations between FLMs' satisfaction with aspects of HR policy and their commitment, satisfaction and motivation.

Commitment is a combination of three questions as is job satisfaction (see Appendix 2 for the detailed questions and the statistical test showing how well they can be combined in a single scale). Motivation was a single question:

◘ How motivated do you feel in your present job?

The most important measures reported here relate to organisational commitment and job satisfaction, in part because they are more reliable through the combination of three questions but mainly because these are associated with higher levels of discretionary behaviour. This discretionary behaviour is sometimes called 'organisation citizenship behaviour', meaning both a willingness to 'go the extra mile' and do things not strictly part of the job, and behaviours which people define as part of their job.

People with higher levels of commitment (technically 'affective commitment' – a wish to stay with your employer) and satisfaction make bigger jobs for themselves and do more. For FLMs a big part of their job is the 'doing' of people management. This is where discretionary behaviour is most likely to be found. There is less room to choose whether or not to undertake those parts of the FLM job concerning the technical and easily measured activities like stock control or meeting daily performance measures.

Table 10 shows where there is an unambiguous connection between satisfaction with a given HR

Table 10 | The relationship between HR policy and practice, satisfaction and attitudinal outcomes for front line managers

HR policies	Organisational commitment	Job satisfaction	Motivation in present job
Performance appraisal	0.346 **	0.409 **	
Training	0.258 **	0.400 **	0.298 **
Career opportunities	0.484 **	0.491 **	0.408 **
Sense of teamworking		0.216 **	
Work–life balance	0.294 **	0.315 **	0.223 **
Rewards and recognition	0.402 **	0.414 **	0.278 **
Communication	0.392 **	0.251 **	0.207 **
Involvement	0.350 **	0.426 **	0. 376 **
Relationship with managers	0.363 **	0.477 **	0.230 **
Management control	0.244 **	0.295 **	
Openness	0.270 **	0.244 **	
Job security	0.270 **		

** significant at 0.01 (2 tailed)
n = 165

policy and the outcome measures of commitment, satisfaction and motivation.

These associations applied pretty well equally to men and women and to those who had been doing the job for a long time, compared with new appointees (although we rarely interviewed someone with less than one year's service). Getting these policies right and applying them such that FLMs are satisfied with how they are appraised, their training and their career opportunity, etc, is clearly worth doing.

A useful way to look at these data is to ask which are the most important policies, and just how important they are. We can do this through regression analysis, which isolates each item to test the extent to which it can be seen as the driver of

commitment and satisfaction. At this stage a lot of policy areas fall out of the running – they may be important in providing an overall impression of supportive HR policy applied to the line, as implied in Table 10, but are not in themselves a strong influence.

The policies and practices that are important for commitment and their relative influence are shown in Figure 7. Five policy and practice areas come out as being particularly important from our survey, and cumulatively they explain just under half of the variance in commitment levels.

Figure 8 does the same analysis with job satisfaction. Here three policy areas in cumulative combination stand out as being especially influential – relationship with managers, career

Figure 7 | The critical determinants of organisational commitment for front line managers

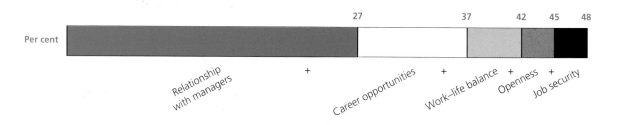

Figure 8 | The critical determinants of job satisfaction for front line managers

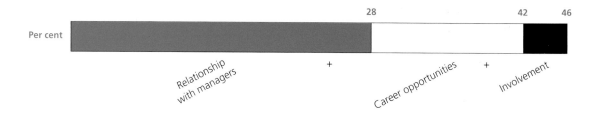

opportunities and involvement. Again, just under half of the variance is explained by these policy means.

Figures 7 and 8 clearly show that by far the largest influence on FLMs' commitment and satisfaction is their relationship with their manager and the management team above them. This explains 27 per cent of commitment and 28 per cent of satisfaction.

Career opportunity is also vitally important. When combined with the relationship with management it explained 37 per cent of commitment and 42 per cent of satisfaction.

In summary, our data shows that the policy mix, or bundle of HR practices, for supporting front line managers is

◘ ensuring good working relationships with their managers

◘ providing career opportunities

◘ supporting their work–life balance

◘ allowing them to participate and feel involved in decisions

◘ having an open organisational culture which allows them to raise a grievance or discuss matters of personal concern

◘ giving them a sense of job security.

> *'... by far the largest influence on FLMs' commitment and satisfaction is their relationship with their manager and the management team ...'*

Relationship with managers

We asked five questions in the survey to do with the relationship employees have with managers – and in this case we mean the relationship of FLMs with their bosses and the higher management in the organisation. As explained in Chapter 2 we combined these to make this one composite variable.

The questions reflected the classic areas of 'doing' or 'being' a manager in managing people. We asked:

◘ How good are managers here at:

– keeping everyone informed about proposed changes?

– providing everyone with a chance to comment on proposals?

– responding to suggestions from employees?

– dealing with problems at the workplace?

– treating employees fairly?

This factor – the FLMs' relationship with their manager and top management generally – was much more important for FLMs than it was for professionals or workers in our companies. This indicates that what makes or breaks FLMs is how well they *themselves* are managed, and how effective the management team is.

There are strong links with organisational values, which played a major part in explaining the success of five of our companies in the main survey and two of the knowledge intensive firms. These 'big ideas', as we called them, provided clear pointers to the type of behaviour expected of managers towards employees, in dealing with each other and in handling customers.

A strong, coherent, easily articulated value statement which reflects and reinforces a set of beliefs gives a clear indication of behaviours that are expected and those that are not tolerated. This is related to 'openness', the extent to which FLMs feel able to raise grievances or discuss problems.

A good example was Selfridges, where the stakeholder value model included statements like 'Selfridges is a very friendly place to work', 'I like my boss and my team', 'I know my opinion and contribution is welcomed', 'I feel welcomed and this makes me welcome others'.

Measuring and monitoring the extent to which employees, and FLMs as a special group, feel these values are achieved, and using the data in performance reviews, is important in making the values real and giving them some priority.

Looking more closely at the relationship with managers it is clear that it was the FLMs' manager who would discuss training and development needs, and how well this was done was a part of building a fruitful relationship between FLMs and top management. This was done more frequently for FLMs – but there were some FLMs who said they had not had such discussions, and we presume that that was because they were not given the opportunity.

70 per cent of FLMs said that their manager helped them to 'some extent' or 'a great extent' in coaching or guiding them (figure 4). This happened much more frequently than for other employees – but some 30 per cent of FLMs nevertheless did not feel that their manager guided them or coached them. This very personal, one-to-one activity is rarely scripted and does not have a distinct time allocation ... yet it is highly valued.

All this raises questions about how good senior managers are at people management, especially when it comes to managing FLMs. A recent study by Whittaker and Marchington (2003) on senior manager roles in HRM concluded (p.259):

Given that HRM is always going to be put into effect by line managers, there needs to be more attention paid to how this group of people is recruited, inducted, appraised and rewarded, and trained in the HR aspects of their jobs. Senior line managers are exceptionally important in the process both in terms of their overt commitment to the development of 'resourceful humans' and in their support for supervisors who attempt to build employee engagement as well as meet short-term business needs.

Career opportunities

Flatter organisations typically found after delayering and organisation redesign pose real challenges both for employees and for FLMs. The gap between the FLM and the next level up can be quite large. In many firms – with the exception of knowledge-based companies which typically recruit only graduates – most FLMs have neither the qualifications nor the experience to gain promotion to a higher level. The gap is too high to jump. These are not the sort of employees who have boundaryless careers. Typically, much of their knowledge and competence is organisation-specific, which makes it harder for them to get an equivalent or better job elsewhere.

Yet our data shows that FLMs who are satisfied with career opportunities provided by their employer respond positively both in terms of their commitment to the firm and in terms of their job satisfaction. Our impression is that people's definition of what they mean by 'career' is often broad-based, including opportunities to do a different job by moving sideways and being provided with training and development to improve their skills and learn new ways of working.

One person we interviewed at Jaguar said she was fully satisfied with her career opportunities but would not take them up because it would be too much of a challenge and would demand greater job stress and disrupt her home–life balance. It was the opportunity that was important to her.

> **'The gap between the FLM and the next level up can be quite large.'**

Looking at all the data, the average level of satisfaction with career opportunities was near the mid-point of the five-point scale at 2.24. This means that around half were satisfied or highly satisfied. One exception was Selfridges, where the team leaders we interviewed were much more satisfied. This is a reflection on the efforts Selfridges made to redesign the role of team leaders and place emphasis on their people management skills and their own development.

Another company with better than average levels of team leader satisfaction with career opportunities was Clerical Medical. Here the emphasis on team-based involvement gave much greater responsibility to team leaders, including Learning and Development Agreements and 360-degree appraisal. The opportunity to discuss their development in their appraisal and the use of a broader-based, more evaluative and developmental appraisal process was linked to this feeling that career opportunities had improved. Team leaders wondered why it had not been done before!

Work–life balance

In an earlier study for the CIPD on the impact of lean methods of working (Hutchinson and Wood, 1999) we noted how, in our case study companies, team leaders – the FLMs – found their jobs stressful and often worried about work at home. This is not necessarily a bad thing, and we know from our study that there is a very strong relationship between organisational commitment and job worry at home, and it is more likely among FLMs. We are fairly convinced that this is because people who are committed to their firm care about what they do and how well they do it, and so tend to think about the job even when not at work.

> *'Involvement in decision-making … was the policy area our FLMs were least happy about, a majority expressing dissatisfaction …'*

And the job an FLM does in terms of managing and leading involves the sort of activity which, unlike some technical work, is something that never ends and in which there is never a 'right' answer.

Our question was not directly about whether those we interviewed felt they had achieved a reasonable balance between home and work, but rather,

- ◘ How well do you feel your company does in helping employees achieve a balance between home life and work?

In other words, our concern was with policy and practice in home–life balance.

There is some evidence that it is very much up to the FLMs' manager to make a reality of home–life balance in the demands made on FLM's, and the

understanding shown by the boss of the pressures being placed on FLMs. This then goes back to the first point – that it is the relationship FLMs have with their boss and senior management which counts.

Clerical Medical came out as particularly good in helping FLMs to achieve a balance between home life and work. This was part of their programme of 'living the brand', which placed special emphasis on 'succeeding through people' and 'people first'.

Involvement in decision-making

This was the policy area our FLMs were least happy about, a majority expressing dissatisfaction with 'How much influence [they had] in company decisions that affect [their] job or work.' This was closely linked to communication – another policy area that on average was a point of concern.

Quite a few FLMs felt that they were kept in the dark and not given opportunities to discuss or influence company policy, and that if they did make suggestions, they were not listened to. One FLM said:

I could jump up and down and scream blue murder, but I don't think it would make much difference in relation to getting new equipment installed – repeated requests are just ignored.

The importance of this is that it is these same people, the FLMs, who are often providing information and leading discussions with their team, trying to solve problems. That is, it is they who provide the employees they are responsible for with opportunities for direct involvement seen in team briefing sessions and team meetings or more formally in such things as Quality Circles. If FLMs feel they are not involved, it is extremely difficult for them to involve their employees – and, as shown in Chapter 3, involvement is important in influencing employee commitment. The frustration shown through our data and our interviews is palpable. The view is, where information and opportunity are not provided,

How can I do my job in leading my team if I do not know what is going on and am not listened to?

There were quite wide differences between the companies in the two studies. One knowledge intensive firm had managed to disillusion FLMs because no information seemed to come down from senior management in this relatively small company. The FLMs were really frustrated, most saying they were extremely dissatisfied with their involvement. Both Jaguar and Selfridges, on the other hand, did better than average.

In the case of Jaguar, group leaders – still classified as manual workers – were a relatively new development at the time of our interviews. A fair number had good working relationships with their immediate boss, the supervisor or superintendent, but some did not. This relationship was of crucial importance, since it was to them they brought team queries, questions and suggestions, and it was the supervisor or superintendent who fed information down and approved decisions.

Managing the managers at Selfridge & Co

Selfridges made a determined and largely successful effort to improve the performance of their FLMs, and this included how the FLMs were themselves managed.

Involvement

When the team leader (TL) job was redefined at Selfridges, all TLs received seven days of training, together, spread over a period of time. This was the first time TLs had got together as a group, and they soon realised they shared common problems and concerns. One consequence of this was the setting up of a team leader forum (at the TL initiative) which now operates in the stores, meeting twice a month. The first monthly meeting is set aside for discussing common issues and problems. At the second (often attended by the operational manager), selected managers are invited to help with relevant problems. For example, an HR specialist might be invited to advise on disciplinary procedure, or recruitment and selection on the floor.

Career opportunities at Selfridges & Co

In staff surveys career opportunities had been identified as an ongoing concern of both the TL population and sales associates. Several positive steps were taken to address these concerns. Firstly, the performance appraisal scheme changed so as to link it more closely to succession planning. Secondly, a 'fast-track' programme was established for sales associates who were identified as having potential for management positions by managers (team leaders and sales managers). Individuals identified as having potential experience a variety of roles – such as deputising for team leaders and 'back of the house' support work – prior to taking on a management role. The programme also benefits staff in so far as it provides networking opportunities.

Training, coaching and development

Assistant sales managers (ASMs) take on the role of coaching or developing team leaders through a variety of formal and informal means. On the formal side, development reviews (see Chapter 3) are conducted twice a year and focus on monitoring team progress against performance indicators such as stock control measures, mystery shopping results, labour turnover, and tidiness and cleanliness of the department. In addition to this, ASMs conduct weekly formal meetings with TLs to assess their training needs, and on a more informal basis do weekly floor walks with the team leader to go over sales and performance issues of Selfridges staff and the concessionaires.

Management support behaviour

One of the most important motivational tools for TLs, acknowledged in our interviews with a selection of their FLMs, is the attitude and behaviour of the senior line manager. As one TL with a good manager remarked:

If you need to talk to her about something, she'll take the time to do it – and that holds a lot for me. And obviously, she's very busy.

If the group leaders were to be effective in leading their team, they could only really do so if they were involved at higher levels and felt they had some influence. Most were, and the group leader 'experiment' was seen as a success and rolled out to the rest of the plant and elsewhere.

Conclusion

Managing managers well, especially FLMs, is vital if they are to go on and lead their teams. We have shown that it is the relationship FLMs have with their boss and senior management generally which makes a difference. Firms like Nationwide, which have strong values clearly articulated and supporting HR policies, are more likely to be successful. These policies include using a competency framework showing a clear understanding of the job FLMs undertake and the behaviours required to be successful. It provides the basis for the measurement of performance and attitudes seen in employee surveys. This then informs the appraisal process, and 360-degree appraisal is found to be particularly useful. A well designed and applied management development scheme links to training opportunities and helps provide a sense of career opportunity – something that is particularly valued by FLMs. The training is focused on leadership skills, and it is here that the coaching and guidance of FLMs by senior managers is particularly helpful.

All these features, including opportunities to be involved in decision-making, increase the level of commitment FLMs show to their firm.

It is this which helps FLMs engage in the sort of discretionary behaviour needed if they are to be effective team leaders.

Some of the companies we studied took particular care in FLM selection, motivation and management, seeing them as the group of employees who made a real difference in the delivery of customer service and in meeting organisational objectives.

This effort in managing the front line managers is vital because it was the FLMs who made the difference in the way employees did their jobs.

Nationwide, after many years of data collection, are unequivocal about this:

Our research has demonstrated that line manager behaviour has a significant impact on employee commitment, which has an impact on customer commitment, which has an impact on business performance.[4]

Endnotes

4   Taken from Ian Lazenby (2003) MBA dissertation on front line leadership.

Chapter 5

◆ Sets out the conclusions that can be drawn about the role of front line managers and their impact on organisational performance

◆ Summarises how organisations might improve the role of front line managers

5 | Practical implications

We have shown in this research that front line managers play a vital role in people management. They do this in a wide variety of ways.

In Chapter 1 we noted how the role of FLMs has become broader as they have taken on more leadership and explicit HR roles in addition to their controlling, monitoring and advisory functions. This often places high demands on them.

In Chapter 2 the importance of the FLM's job in people management was seen in the ways their team members, or those they managed, reacted in terms of commitment to their employer, their satisfaction with their job and their level of motivation. The relationship staff have with their managers, and FLMs particularly, was shown to be often the most important factor influencing these attitudes, or one of the most important.

Older workers and those who had worked in a firm for a number of years were more sceptical than younger, newer workers, but the associations remain. It is these positive attitudes which are seen to be linked to discretionary behaviour – the essential requirement for people to work effectively, especially when they are in jobs which require doing something extra or better to improve performance.

Two particular factors were highlighted in Chapter 2. First, the level of job discretion an individual has in how he or she does his or her job is strongly influenced by FLMs. That is, it is these managers who can permit and encourage people to be responsible for their own job, or can stifle this through more controlling or autocratic behaviour.

One aspect here, examined in Chapter 3, is the way and the extent to which FLMs provide coaching and guidance for their employees, usually on a one-to-one basis.

Second, as team leaders – as they were in most of our companies – FLMs were crucial in making teams effective. There were very strong associations between staff views or their sense of teamworking and their views on how effective teamworking was and their rating of their relationship with managers.

In sum, our research shows that FLMs:

◘ need to build a good working relationship with their staff, especially by leading, listening, asking, communicating, being fair, responding to suggestions and dealing with problems

◘ can help employees take greater responsibility for how they do their jobs, for example with coaching and guidance

◘ are essential in building effective teams.

> *'... no one else can. This is why one of our firms ... referred to the importance of "bringing policies to life" as one of the roles of front line managers.'*

In Chapter 3 we looked explicitly at the key policy areas in people management where FLMs made a difference. Six policy areas came out as particularly important. These are:

◘ performance appraisal

◘ training, coaching and guidance

◘ involvement and communication

◘ openness – how easy is it for employees to discuss matters with their FLM?

◘ work–life balance

◘ recognition – the extent to which employees feel their contribution is recognised.

All these activities are classic areas of HR in which good organisations, like those we studied, have clear policies that are revised from time to time. These cannot, of course, be delivered by the HR department. Although they need the support of senior line management, it is only the FLMs and

their immediate superiors who can ensure that they are delivered. No one else can. This is why one of our firms (Tesco) referred to the importance of 'bringing policies to life' as one of the roles of FLMs.

How can organisations improve the quality of their FLMs in people management? We discussed in chapter 3 some of the difficulties FLM's have in delivering HR policy and practices. A number of points emerge from Chapter 4 on how FLMs are themselves managed.

◘ FLMs need time to carry out their people management roles. There is a tendency for these 'soft' parts of managing to be driven out in favour of other management duties, such as controlling, budgeting and monitoring. On occasions they also have to cover for absent team members.

◘ They need to be carefully selected, with more attention paid to behaviour competencies. One of our companies, Selfridges, has done this with beneficial results.

◘ They need the support of strong organisational values which give emphasis to the fundamentals of people management and show clearly those leadership behaviours expected, and those not permitted.

◘ They need a good working relationship with their managers. This was by far the most important factor influencing the FLMs' own levels of commitment to the organisation. 360-degree appraisal was especially important here.

- They need to receive sufficient skills training to enable them to perform their people management activities, such as communication skills, handling discipline and grievances.

- They need a sense of career opportunity, and this is linked to training and development. If they feel stuck in a dead-end job with little support from their bosses, the drop in commitment is huge.

- They need a sense of involvement in decision-making if they too are to involve their team and team members.

- They need a sense of job security and a feeling that they can discuss matters with their managers. Part of this is being treated with respect.

A generation ago it was common to talk about the 'forgotten supervisors', the layer of staff who are not really managers, no longer just workers but stuck in the middle and often neglected. Much has changed since then in many organisations – but there is still much to be done to give FLMs the attention, the respect, the training and the policy tools they need to deliver, through people management, better employment relations and higher performance.

Good management of FLMs is a crucial part of understanding how people management impacts on organisational performance.

Appendix 1 | Case study organisations – brief profiles

Ait

Ait is a software organisation engaged in the production of information systems solutions for around 20 clients mostly in the financial services sector. Established in 1986 by four employees, they have been a plc since 1997, although their status has recently changed and they are now listed on the alternative investment market. At the time of our research they employed around 400 people in Henley-on-Thames, Britain's own 'silicon valley', where the market for experienced, skilled staff is very tight.

The product market is intensely competitive and the technology is changing rapidly.
Work is organised around the idea of multiple teams and multiple roles. All employees belong to at least two teams, and professional employees belong to three – and this endeavours to overcome the normal functional boundary problems found in many larger organisations. Operational teams are based around projects for particular clients and include various specialists under a project manager or director. Vocational teams bring together specialists – eg testers or business analysts – and T-

groups provide a means of upward and downward communication for all employees.

Our interviews for the employee attitude survey focused on two project teams. We interviewed 36 non-managerial staff in year 1 (such as developers, systems analysts and testers) and 33 in year 2.

(However, as noted earlier, since the period of our research ait has undergone a number of substantial changes, although the basis of the policies and procedures described here is still in place.)

Clerical Medical

At the time of this study Clerical Medical employed around 2,000 staff. It is one of the largest financial services providers in the UK, operating mainly through independent financial advisers. Clerical Medical is now part of the HBOS Group created after the merger of the Halifax group and Bank of Scotland. The HBOS Group is one of the largest financial services groups in Europe. Clerical Medical is part of its insurance and investment division.

Our unit of analysis was customer services, where we focused on four departments: new business services, corporate and executive pensions, final salary, and annuities. During the course of our research there was a lot of emphasis placed on improving customer services through a number of HR initiatives, including 'living the brand', a campaign aimed to link individual jobs with the direction of the organisation and improved customer service, and changes at team leader and management level.

For our attitude survey we interviewed 29 people in year 1 and 34 in year 2, the majority of whom were senior administrators and administrators.

Contact 24

Contact 24, based in Bristol, is a call and contact centre which, since September 2000, has been owned by Havas, a large French-based advertising and communication organisation. Contact 24 provides contact and call centre services for a wide range of clients including supermarkets, car manufacturers and financial services organisations. It employs around 950 personnel (excluding temporary employees) on two sites, and also provides a managed service activity on two other sites for outside clients.

Contact 24 offers its clients a variety of services. Dedicated contracts have been increasing recently and involve teams of customer service representatives (CSRs) working exclusively for one client. With the exception of the small bureau that carries out tactical work for a range of clients, the call centres are organised in client teams, ranging from 200 to 20 employees.

The organisation works closely with many clients to ensure that the CSRs who work on dedicated project teams are those most suitable for the particular service or product offered. Customer demand varies in often unpredictable ways, creating pressure on managing appropriate staffing levels.

Our employee interviews focused on CSRs from one call centre site, working for four client teams, where we interviewed 33 in year 1 and 40 in year 2. The majority of these employees were young (55 per cent were under 30 years of age) and had very short job tenure (only 25 per cent, for example, had worked for the organisation for two years or more) – a fairly typical profile for a call centre workforce.

Jaguar Cars

Jaguar Cars have seen a revival in growth in recent years, resulting in the launch of new models and substantial expansion of manufacturing capacity. Much of this was down to the success of a number of quality initiatives launched in the 1990s, many of which were driven by Ford, who took over the organisation in 1989. Today, Jaguar has three sites, Browns Lane, Coventry, Castle Bromwich, and the new, revitalised old Ford plant at Halewood.

Our research was conducted at the Browns Lane plant in Coventry. We interviewed 41 manual workers in the first year, mainly from the trim and assembly workshop, and 37 in the second year.

Nationwide Building Society

Employing around 13,500 staff, (FTE) the Nationwide is the country's largest building society, providing a broad range of financial products and services for over 10 million members, including mortgages, savings, current accounts, life assurance, personal loans and household insurance. In recent years Nationwide has become well known for its commitment to mutuality, and as more and more building societies convert to plc status this characteristic of ownership has come to distinguish them in the marketplace and been used to their competitive advantage.

The unit of analysis chosen for our study was the sales force for the southern region, which at the time of our first interviews in July 2000 employed 46 financial consultations (FCs), 44 of whom were interviewed on a structured basis for the employee attitude survey in year 1. By the time of our second survey the sales force had grown, and 49 were interviewed in year 2. The sales force covers a large geographical area encompassing a wide variety of customer needs.

Labour turnover for financial consultants was about 5 per cent – much lower than the industry average – and in our sample just under half (41 per cent) had worked for the Nationwide for 10 years or more.

Oxford Magnet Technology

Oxford Magnet Technology (OMT) designs and manufactures superconducting magnets and is a jointly-owned subsidiary of Siemens and Oxford Instruments. Siemens owns a controlling interest in the firm, but allows complete discretion in operation. This is important to the market position of OMT. Approximately two thirds of the business conduced by OMT is for Siemens, but the remaining one third is for a range of other clients.

OMT makes superconductive magnets for use in magnetic resonance imaging (MRI) equipment. The production process is quite involved, and can take as long as 28 days to complete, depending on the magnet being produced. Unfortunately, it is largely impossible to test a magnet during this production process, and so there is a substantial investment in work in progress by the time any magnet reaches the test phase.

Our unit of analysis in OMT consisted of staff surrounding two magnet projects. The attitude survey covered 40 members of the magnet design teams as well as those involved in the assembly of these two products in both years 1 and 2.

PricewaterhouseCoopers (PWC)

At the time of our first interviews PricewaterhouseCoopers (PWC) was still readjusting from the merger between Price Waterhouse and Coopers which took place in July 1998. Our research focused on one of the five lines of services known as ABAS (Assurance and Business Advisory Services), the main business activity of which is to conduct audits and provide assurance for clients on their business.

We looked at three offices in the southern region of ABAS – Southampton, Reading and Uxbridge – interviewing senior associates, assistant managers and managers for the employee attitude survey. In year 1 we interviewed 43 employees, but in year 2 this fell to 27 due to a reorganisation of the ABAS line of business which affected the offices we were studying and made it difficult for us to make a realistic comparison between the two years.

The Royal Mint

At the time of our research the Royal Mint employed around 1,000 staff in the manufacture of circulation coins, collector coinages, coin blanks and medals for both UK and overseas customers. Although the organisation had had market dominance for much of its working life, during the latter half of the 1990s the trading environment began to change with increased overseas competition, higher customer demands and the threat of the loss of some traditional overseas markets. At the same time, however, the introduction of the single European currency afforded new market opportunities in the form of the euro and the potential for considerable growth. As a result, major investment took place in capital equipment and new working practices were introduced with an emphasis on quality, flexibility and teamworking.

The unit of analysis was one of the production departments known as MRB (melting, rolling and blanking), where the first stage of the coining process takes place. The workforce here comprises long-serving employees (81 per cent had worked for the Mint for 10 years or more) who were heavily unionised (91 per cent were members of a union). Employees in this area had been top earners in the Mint over the previous 25 years – and had one of the worst employee relations in the organisation. We interviewed 42 operatives in year 1 and 33 in year 2. (Unfortunately major changes were taking place during the second year, which prevented us from conducting the full number of interviews.)

Royal United Hospital, Bath (RUH)

The RUH is a district general hospital employing around 3,500 staff on a single site in Bath. It was a first-wave Trust, achieving trust status in 1992. Like many NHS hospitals it has been through turbulent times. Five years ago it suffered a financial crisis and brought in a new chief executive who introduced radical changes leading to national recognition and increased funding. However, during the course of our research the Trust suffered further difficulties because of problems with meeting performance targets, changes in the top management team and bad publicity in the press.

Our research focused on one clinical department where we interviewed 40 staff in the first year and 39 in the second year for our attitude survey.

This covered a range of non-managerial jobs both on and off the wards, including nurses, HCAs, administrative staff, technicians and porters.

Selfridges Plc

The Selfridges story is one of corporate renewal where people management has played a vital role in creating a highly successful and expanding up-market retail department store. Widely described as the embodiment of Grace Brothers in the 1980s and early 1990s, it began the process of renewal and growth in the mid-1990s with the appointment of new management, especially the visionary chief executive, Vittorio Radice.

In 1998 Selfridges de-merged from the Sears Group and opened up a new UK store at Trafford Park, Manchester. Subsequently, in 2002 another store has been opened in Manchester city centre, and the Birmingham store will open in 2003.

Selfridges trades as the 'house of brands', and as a consequence a high proportion of sales associates are concessionary staff – in other words, staff not employed by Selfridges at all but by the brand organisation with a concession to sell their products in the store. At Trafford Park, for example, some 200 of 450 staff are concessionary staff. To the customer, however, these staff appear to be Selfridges' own staff. In addition there is a heavy reliance on part-time staff (65 per cent at Trafford Centre). These characteristics obviously present challenges in terms of managing the workforce.

The unit of analysis was the Manchester store at Trafford Park, and we focused on two departments – ladieswear and household. We interviewed 40 sales associates in year 1 and 41 in year 2. Of these, 95 per cent were women and half were under 30 years of age. Given that the store had only been open for a few years, the length of service was usually less than two years.

Siemens Medical Solutions

Siemens Medical Solutions is a wholly-owned subsidiary of Siemens AG. It is a market leader, employing 550 staff in the UK, and provides a wide range of high-technology medical capital equipment, IT solutions and managed technology services for the NHS and private healthcare sector. The division of the organisation we focused on was Technical Customer Services, which deals with the installation, commission and servicing of all medical equipment made by Siemens, including MRI body-scanners incorporating magnets from OMT.

Our employee attitude survey centred on one of five regions – the South-West and Wales region – and comprised regional service engineers as well as the engineers engaged in the provision of UK technical support and customer service representatives. The technical support team and national call centre staff are based at the UK headquarters for Siemens in Bracknell, while regional service engineers are home-based but are co-ordinated and despatched by the UK call centre.

In total 27 employees were interviewed in year 1 only.

Tesco Stores

Tesco, the largest supermarket chain in the UK, employed (in 1999/2000) around 170,000 staff in 659 stores across the country. The organisation underwent considerable change in the mid-1990s in order to improve its competitive position, with a much greater emphasis on a customer-facing culture. Through a policy of improving customer service and lowering prices Tesco has successfully increased its market share in recent years, although the industry has seen very little growth.

One of the characteristics of Tesco which particularly attracted us to this organisation for research purposes was the operation of highly standardised policies, procedures and processes across all stores, including HR policies.

Our research focused on four stores in a single region. All were in market towns with similar socio-economic profiles. Our interviews for the employee attitude survey were with the section manager population (a first line manager's position). In year 1 we interviewed 43 section managers, representing two thirds of the section manager population in those stores; and in year 2 we interviewed 40 section managers.

Appendix 2 | Variables used in statistical analysis

Outcomes

Commitment (Alpha = 0.7345)

- ◘ 'I feel proud to tell people who I work for'

- ◘ 'I feel loyal to my company'

- ◘ 'I share the values of my company'

Job satisfaction (Alpha = 0.6302)

- ◘ 'How satisfied are you with the amount of influence you have over your job?'

- ◘ 'How satisfied are you with the sense of achievement you get from your job?'

- ◘ 'How satisfied are you with the respect you get?'

Motivation

- ◘ 'How motivated do you feel in your present job?'

Effort (Alpha = 0.6459)

- ◘ 'My job requires me to work hard'

- ◘ 'I never seem to have enough time to get my job done'

- ◘ '… not enough time for my job'

- ◘ '… worry about outside working hours'

HR variables

Relationship with managers (Alpha = 0.8622)

'How good are managers at:

- ◘ keeping everyone informed about proposed changes?

- ◘ providing everyone with a chance to comment on proposal?

- ◘ responding to suggestions from employees?

- ◘ dealing with problems at the workplace?

- ◘ treating employees fairly?'

Rewards and recognition (Alpha = 0.733)

- ◘ 'How satisfied do you feel with your pay?'

- ◘ 'How satisfied are you with your pay, compared with the pay of other people that work here?'

◘ 'Overall, how satisfied do you feel with the rewards and recognition you receive for your performance?'

◘ 'How satisfied do you feel with the benefits you receive – other than pay?'

Communication (Alpha = 0.6547)

◘ 'How satisfied do you feel with the amount of information you receive about how your company is performing?'

◘ 'I am fully aware of how I contribute to the company's achieving its business objectives'

◘ 'Everyone here is well aware of the long-term plans and goals of the organisation'

Performance appraisal

◘ 'How satisfied are you with this method of appraising your performance?'

Training

◘ 'How satisfied do you feel with the level of training you receive in your current job?'

Career opportunities

◘ 'Overall, how satisfied do you feel with your current career opportunities?'

Teamworking

◘ 'Describe the sense of teamworking in your work groups'

Work–life balance

◘ 'How well do you feel that your company does in helping employees achieve a balance between home life and work?'

Involvement

◘ 'Overall, how satisfied are you with the influence you have in company decisions that affect your job or work?'

Openness

◘ 'To what extent do you feel that your company provides you with reasonable opportunities to express grievances and raise personal concerns?'

Job security

◘ 'I feel that my job is secure'

Note on statistical produres: Reliability of variables used

Cronbach's Alpha reliability coefficient is used to measure the degree of consistency between multiple measures of variable. Good consistency is when the result is 0.8 and above. However in exploratory research, which is the approach taken in this study, a figure of 0.6 and above is considered acceptable.

References

Bond, S. and Wise, S. (2003)

'Family leave policies and devolution to the line', *Personnel Review*, Vol. 32 No. 1 pp.58–72.

Boxall, P. and Purcell, J. (2003)

Strategy and Human Resource Management. London, Palgrave.

Carroll, S. J. and Schneier, C. E. (1982)

Performance Appraisal and Review Systems: The identification, measurement and development of performance in organisations. Glenview, IL, Scott Foresam.

Cully, M., Woodland, S., O'Reilly, A. and Dix, G. (1999)

Britain at Work. London, Routledge.

Fenton O'Creevy, M. (2001)

'Employee involvement and the middle manager: saboteur or scapegoat?', *Human Resource Management Journal*, Vol. 11, No. 1, pp.24–40.

Geary, J. F and Dobbins, A. (2001)

'Teamworking: a new dynamic in the pursuit of management control', *Human Resource Management Journal*, Vol. 11, No. 1, pp.3–29.

Grint, K. (1993)

'What's wrong with performance appraisal? A critique and suggestions', *Human Resource Management Journal*, 3(3), pp.61–77.

Guest, D. E. (1991)

'Personnel management: the end of orthodoxy?', *British Journal of Industrial Relations*, 29(2), pp.149–176.

Harris, L. (2001)

'Rewarding employee performance: line managers' values, beliefs and perspectives', *The International Journal of Human Resource Management*, Vol. 12, No. 7.

Hutchinson, S., Kinnie, N., Purcell, J., Collinson, M., Terry, M. and Scarborough, H.

'Getting fit, staying fit, developing lean and responsive organisation'. London, CIPD.

Hutchinson, S. and Wood, S. (1995)

'The UK experience' in *Personnel and the Line: Developing the New Relationship*. London, IPD.

Larsen, H. H. and Brewster, C. (2003)

'Line management responsibility for HRM: what is happening in Europe?', *Employee Relations*, Vol. 25, No. 3, pp.228–244.

Lawler, E. E. III (1994)

'Performance management: the next generation', *Compensation and Benefits Review*, May-June, pp.16–28.

Marchington, M. (2001)

'Employee involvement at work', in J. Storey (ed.) *Human Resource Management: A critical text*, 2nd edition. London, Thomson.

Maslow, A. (1954)

'A theory of human motivation', *Psychological Review*, Vol. 50, pp.370–396.

McGovern, P., Gratton, L., Hope-Hailey, V., Stiles, P. and Truss, C. (1997)

'Human resource management on the line?', *Human Resource Management Journal*, Vol. 7, No. 4, pp.12–29.

Pil, F. and MacDuffie, J. (1996)

'The adoption of high-involvement work practices', *Industrial Relations*, 35, 3, pp.423–455.

Purcell, J., Kinnie, N., Hutchinson, S., Rayton, B. and Swart, J. (2003)

Understanding the People and Performance Link: Unlocking the black box. London, CIPD.

Redman, T. (2001)

'Performance appraisal', in T. Redman and A. Wilkinson (eds) *Contemporary Human Resource Management*. Harlow, Pearson Education.

Renwick, D. (2002)

'Line manager involvement in HRM: an inside view', *Employee Relations*, Vol. 35, No. 3, pp.262–280.

Snape, E., Redman, T. and Bamber, G. (1994)

Managing Managers. Oxford, Blackwells.

Swart, J., Kinnie, N. and Purcell, J. (2003)

People and Performance in Knowledge Intensive Firms. London, CIPD.

Whittaker, S. and Marchington, M. (2003)

'Devolving HR responsibility to the line: threat, opportunity or partnership?', *Employee Relations*, Vol. 25, No. 3, pp.245–261.